IS HE CHEATING ON YOU?

829 Telltale Signs

IS HE CHEATING ON YOU?

829 Telltale Signs

by

Ruth Houston

Lifestyle Publications

ISBN: 0-9720553-4-7
Printed in the United States of America
Cover design and Layout: Hiram Adu-Kusi

Published by

LIFESTYLE PUBLICATIONS
P.O. Box 730797
Elmhurst, New York 11373
(800) 585-4905
fax (718) 592-2018
E-mail: IsHeCheatingBook@aol.com

WEB SITES
LifestylePublications.com
IsHeCheatingOnYou.com

You may order this book directly from the publisher at the address
above, through our toll-free number or by visiting one of our web
sites. Or you may use an order blank from the back of this book.

Dedication

This book is dedicated to Daisy Miller - my mother, my confidante, my very best friend. Without her love, wisdom, care and concern, I would never have survived the trauma and the devastation of having been a victim of infidelity.

Unfortunately she did not live to see me fulfill my dream of writing a book to help the millions of other women who are victims of infidelity. It would have pleased her immensely to know that this book finally became a reality, and that her daughter is now happily married to a man who shares the same values on the sanctity of marriage.

"Let marriage be honorable among all,
and the marriage bed be without defilement,
for God will judge fornicators and adulterers."

Hebrews 13:4, New World Translation

TABLE OF CONTENTS

PART THREE

DISCLAIMER

This publication is designed to give accurate and authoritative information with regard to the subject matter covered. It is sold with the understanding that the publisher and author are not engaged in rendering legal, accounting, or other professional advice. If legal advice or other expert assistance is required, the services of a competent professional should be sought.

Every effort has been made to make this publication as complete and as accurate as possible with respect to the subject matter covered. However there *may be mistakes,* both typographical and in content. Therefore this text should be used only as a general guide.

The purpose of this publication is to educate and inform. The author and Lifestyle Publications shall have neither liability nor responsibility to any person or entity with respect to any loss or damage caused, or alleged to have been caused, directly or indirectly, by the information contained in this book.

If you do not wish to be bound by the above, you may return this book to the publisher for a full refund.

ACKNOWLEDGEMENTS

I would like to acknowledge the following people whose support, assistance, and words of encouragement were instrumental in the completion of this book:

My husband, Manley, for his unfailing love, support, encouragement and unwavering confidence in my ability to make this book a reality.

My sister LuVonne, for her love, her gentle prodding, her valuable feedback and for taking this project more seriously than anyone else.

Priscilla, Sarah and Sonia, for being there for me during the aftermath of my (now ex-)husband's affair.

Chrissy, for brainstorming with me during the early stages of this book.

Mommy Maude and Daddy Morris, who patiently endured being deprived of their weekly phone calls while this book was being written.

Our 9 cats, who kept me company during my midnight marathon writing sessions.

Chandra, my editor– even though I stubbornly ignored some of her suggestions.

Hiram, for his dedication, his resourcefulness, and his graphic arts skills which were essential to the layout and cover design of this book.

MaryAnn, whose suggestions helped us fine tune the cover design.

Poly, who performed miracles when our computer system went down.

Robin, for making sure we had the right software to complete this project.

Ceteria, Pam and Cheryl, for willingly volunteering to read the manuscript in its early stages.

The Adu-Kusi family, for putting up with me for long hours while I worked on the layout with their son.

Nancy, Estelle, and all the members of the Sister's Circle for patiently listening to my "joys and concerns" as this book progressed.

The staff and clients at Housing Works who had to listen to my husband Manley for months as he extolled the virtues of "his wife's book."

The dozens of women who said – "Write it – I'll buy it and I'll recommend it to all my friends."

To all the other friends, neighbors, family members, and acquaintances too numerous to mention, who played a part, however small, in the completion of this book.

And last, but certainly not least, I acknowledge Jehovah God for giving me the insight and the ability to share this information with the women who need it most.

*"Let marriage be honorable among all,
and the marriage bed be without
defilement, for God will judge
fornicators and adulterers."*

Hebrews 13:4, New World Translation

INTRODUCTION

The day I discovered my husband, Frank was cheating on me is forever etched in my mind. I will never forget my bewilderment, shock, confusion and my uncertainty about what to do next. I was totally devastated, and asked myself over and over "How could I have missed all the signs?"

I accidentally stumbled onto Frank's infidelity while taping telephone interviews from my home office for an article assignment. I took a break from my work and returned to find that I'd inadvertently taped an incriminating phone call from Frank to Michelle, made from our bedroom extension.

That Frank might be cheating on me was the farthest thing from my mind, even though his behavior had been a little unusual the past few months. When infidelity did cross my mind, it was just a fleeting thought – one I dismissed as quickly as it occurred. It was so far-fetched that I didn't give it serious consideration. Frank and I had a good marriage (or so I thought). Friends, family – even strangers, (male and female) often commented on what a "perfect couple" we were. The relationship articles and "Good Loving" column I wrote appeared regularly in women's magazines and earned me frequent guest spots on radio talk shows. Our marriage (a second for me and a third for Frank) was the envy of all our friends. Still, I was at a loss to explain some of the odd things Frank had recently said and done. Nothing major – just a number of little things that were out of character for him and didn't seem to make sense. I finally chalked it up to male menopause (he was nearing 50) or stress from the heavy overtime he'd been working .

During the weeks that followed, I discovered that Frank had not one, but three lovers. I was totally dumb-founded when I learned about his weekend morning "quickies" with Alexis, his early departures from work for afternoon trysts with Michelle, Marlene's weekend stay at our apartment while I was away on business trips and more. Worst of all, these things had taken place right under my very nose.

In light of the things I discovered, I now saw Frank's behavior through different eyes. And I became keenly aware of all the telltale signs I'd missed. A lot of the strange things Frank did suddenly began to make sense.

One day I overheard Frank say he'd attended a birthday party his friend Max had given for his girlfriend. That was the only thing I heard. Since I knew Max's wife Wendy, I passed this nugget of information on to her. Working this lone piece of information, Wendy conducted what I consider to be a masterpiece of detective work. In less than 3 weeks, she managed to find out the name of Max's girlfriend, her phone number and address, the address and phone number of her job, and was able to pinpoint approximately how long the affair had been going on. Wendy also found out where and when the birthday party had been given, how much it cost, the names of several guests in attendance, and verified that Max had indeed "footed the bill". She even confiscated a gift Max had hidden in the trunk of his car.

Since Wendy and Max co-owned a business, she immediately took steps to protect herself financially. She transferred the bulk of their joint funds to a separate account – much to the surprise (and embarrassment) of Max when he attempted to withdraw funds behind Wendy's back. Their marriage survived – largely because instead of allowing herself to become a victim, Wendy actively searched for confirming telltale signs. She found them early enough to take positive action and get her marriage back on track.

Though there were other factors involved, my marriage failed, to a large degree, because I was oblivious to the early warning signs. Being a naturally trusting person, I'd missed most of the telltale signs, despite the fact that they were staring me in the face. I could have saved myself a lot of headaches, heartaches and anguish if I'd realized the significance of those signs when they first appeared. Yet, my marriage was not unique in this respect. It was one of the millions of marriages impacted by extramarital affairs, where the wife is the "last to know.".

As I struggled to make sense of what was happening and find solutions, I began researching the topic of infidelity. I had no idea how to handle the situation and ended up doing all the wrong things My research led to a series of articles based on information gleaned from leading marriage and family therapists. Although I gained a wealth of knowledge on recognizing and coping with infidelity, for me, this knowledge came too late. Frank and I eventually got a divorce. But I vowed that once I recovered from the trauma of that experience, I'd share what I learned with other women in similar situations.

The statistics on infidelity are astounding. The most widely accepted figures indicate that between 50 and 70 percent of married men (between 38 and 53 million men) have cheated or will cheat on their wives. One study found that 70 percent of the women whose husbands were cheating did not know about their husband's affair. Of the millions of women who are either victims or potential victims of infidelity, between 26 and 37 million of those women did not (or will not) recognize the telltale signs. Yet the media tends to treat infidelity as a form of entertainment. Movies, novels, soap operas, talk shows, gossip columns and women's magazines continue to dramatize, analyze and glamorize extramarital affairs. Few people other than its victims take it seriously.

This book is the first in a series information products (books, booklets and tapes) on infidelity based on my personal experience and nearly 9 years of research on this topic.   I've read hundreds of accounts of infidelity, interviewed scores of women about their personal experiences and the experiences of women they know. I've surfed the Net checking out websites, chat rooms and forums devoted to infidelity and related issues.   **"Is He Cheating on You? – 829 Telltale Signs"** is the book I wish I'd had when those first telltale signs began to crop up in my marriage. If I'd recognized those signs early on, things might have had a different ending.

This book is my way of sharing what I learned about infidelity with other women facing this traumatic situation. Unsuspecting women need an easy-to-use, reliable, inexpensive tool to help them find out the truth   because millions of acts of infidelity go undetected.

Knowledge is power and I firmly believe every woman should learn to recognize the telltale signs. There's nothing worse than not knowing – or being the last to know. If you don't know what's going on, it's impossible for you to protect yourself or do anything   about it. Rather than making conscious decisions about what to do, you'll be swept along with the tide.

On the other hand, if you know what's happening, you stand a fighting chance of being able to nip the situation in the bud. More importantly, you can take steps to prepare yourself mentally, financially and legally for the possibility that your marriage may end. At least you won't be the "last one to know".

Is He Cheating on You? is not just for wives who suspect their husbands of cheating. It's also for unsuspecting wives who have no idea that an affair might be taking place. It's full of simple, straight-forward, solid information that no woman should be without. Armed with nothing more than your eyes, your ears, this book and your personal knowledge of your husband, it will be easy for you recognize the telltale signs.

It is my sincere hope that this book will open the eyes of the millions of unsuspecting women who have no idea their husbands are cheating on them. The purpose of this book is not to make women suspicious of their husbands. It was written to make women aware of the telltale signs that indicate the possibility of an affair. Every woman deserves to know the truth. No woman should find herself in the unfortunate position of being "the last to know."

To those of you who suspect your husband of cheating, I implore you - for your own peace of mind, for your physical health (think HIV/AIDS and STDs), for your mental and emotional well-being, and for your future financial well-being as well – find out if what you suspect is true. Don't speculate – investigate!

Ruth Houston

NOTE: Despite my traumatic experience with Frank, this story does have a happy ending. I've been happily married (almost 3 years now) to a man who also values the sanctity of marriage as highly as I do. (Ironically, he too, was cheated on, with disastrous results.)

*Frank, Marlene, Michelle, Alexis, Max and Wendy are not their real names. For legal reasons, the names have been changed to protect the guilty as well as the innocent.

PART I

Chapter 1

IS HE CHEATING?

Three out of four men have cheated or will cheat on their mates. Do those statistics surprise you? Family therapist Frank Pittman surmises that there are probably as many acts of infidelity in our society as there are traffic accidents. Men cheat on their mates far more often than people are willing to admit. Yet if you stop to think about it, almost everyone knows someone who has had or is having an affair.

Infidelity is now so common that it is hard to pinpoint exactly how widespread it is. Though statistics vary, the most widely accepted figures indicate that between 50% and 70% of all married men have cheated on their wives. A study conducted by the psychology department of the University of Michigan puts that estimate as high as 75%. Other studies reveal that 84% of American men cheat. So we can safely say that approximately three out of every four men cheat on their wives.

Somewhere between 38 and 53 million women are likely to become victims of infidelity at some point in their lives. One study further revealed that two-thirds of the men who were cheating admitted to having had more than one affair; 25% of these men actually had four or more affairs during their marriage. Statistics like these are hard to ignore.

Any Woman Can Be a Victim

Don't sit back and think it could never happen to you. Infidelity has no boundaries. You could be its next victim. In fact, you could unknowingly be a victim right now. Infidelity does not discriminate. It can affect couples of any race, creed, or color. Rich or poor, young or old, newlywed or approaching your fiftieth anniversary, infidelity can happen to anyone - including you. We accept that infidelity can rear its ugly head in troubled marriages. But it may surprise you to learn that it can occur in happy relationships too. No one is immune.

Despite the fact that an overwhelming majority of men cheat on their mates, much of this cheating goes undetected. There's a lot of truth to that saying: "The wife is always the last to know." According to one study, 70% of married women whose husbands were cheating had no idea their husbands were having an affair. We're talking about at least 26 million women who failed to recognize the telltale signs.

It Takes a Tragic Toll

Infidelity has reached epidemic proportions. It takes a tragic emotional, physical, and financial toll on the lives of all those it touches. The statistics only hint at the devastation it leaves in its wake: divorce, broken homes, troubled children, domestic violence, murder, suicide, HIV/AIDS and other sexually transmitted diseases (STDs). Hidden in those statistics are the oceans of tears shed, endless days spent in anguish, countless sleepless nights, the immeasurable confusion, grief, anxiety, heart-wrenching pain and a profound sense of betrayal and shattered trust. In short, infidelity can wreak havoc in many lives. It's one of the leading causes of divorce.

Trust Your Intuition

No doubt you're reading this book because you suspect your husband of cheating on you. The thought of this probably haunts you day and night. You may have nothing more to go on at this point other than a "nagging feeling" that something's not quite right. You may have even questioned your husband only to have him make you feel guilty about your suspicions. Don't be so quick to dismiss your intuition. It may not be all in your mind. According to statistics, 85% of women who felt their husband was cheating turned out to be right. If you're in doubt, it can't hurt to things out. Don't speculate - investigate

With the prevalence of HIV/AIDS and other STDs, can you afford to put yourself at risk by ignoring the possibility of your husband having an affair? You need to know for sure. Instead of speculating, do a little investigating. If, after checking things out, it turns out you are wrong, you can at least put your mind at ease. If it turns out your husband really is cheating on you, you can take whatever steps are necessary for your financial, emotional and physical well-being. Your future rests on being able to prove or disprove what you suspect.

Affairs usually unfold in stages. With the exception of a one-night stand, a man rarely goes from faithful spouse one day to cheating husband the next. There are usually telltale signs along the way. A man will display these signs regardless of whether he's actually having an affair or laying the groundwork for having one.

What About Hiring a Detective?

If you suspect your husband of cheating on you, how can you find out for sure? You could hire a detective to verify your suspicions, but it would cost considerably more than the price of this book. Investigation fees range from $50 or more per hour, with a three- or four-hour minimum. They can easily end up costing hundreds or thousands. Maybe you're reluctant (and rightly so) to invest that kind of money at this stage. Even if money is no object, it's not advisable to hire an investigator yet. Why pay someone to find out something you can easily discover yourself? Many telltale signs are things that only you, as a wife, are in a position to detect. You're better off doing some preliminary checking to see what you can find out on your own.

This book will tell you exactly how to gather information on your own for a fraction of what it would cost you to hire a detective. The telltale signs listed here don't require any special equipment or skills to detect. In fact, you won't need anything other than your eyes and ears, your personal knowledge of your husband and an awareness of the signs in this book. Once you know what to look for, the signs are easy to find. All you have to do is stay alert.

Before seeking the services of a private detective, do some sleuthing of your own. Your initial findings will determine if further investigation is needed. Once you've done the preliminary legwork, you can turn things over to a professional, if you desire. A detective can monitor your husband's activities, verify your findings and obtain additional details you may have been unable to get on your own. He can also provide you with documented proof for legal action. And having done much of the detective work yourself will insure that your detective fees are kept to a minimum.

Find Out the Truth With This Book

Is he cheating on you? I sincerely hope not, having been a victim of infidelity myself. But this book will help you find out if he is. It's the kind of book I searched for when I suspected my (now ex-) husband of cheating on me. But there was nothing like it available at the time. *Is He Cheating on You?* is a comprehensive guide to more than 800 telltale signs – the obvious (and not so obvious) signs of a husband who's cheating – or planning to cheat – on his wife. This book should be "required reading" if you suspect your husband of having an affair. (Just keep it out of his sight.) It will save you countless hours of wondering and many sleepless nights. It will even help you detect the early warning signs of a budding affair, because a man who's just toying with the idea of cheating also leaves telltale signs behind. If you find out early enough, you may be able to stop the affair before it begins.

The telltale signs are grouped into twenty-one categories:

- Physical Appearance
- How He Relates to You
- Conversational Clues
- Work Habits
- Day-to-Day Behavior
- Financial Affairs
- Travel
- Personality or Behavioral Changes
- Absences
- Telephone Tip-offs
- Car Clues
- Sex
- Eating Habits
- Smells and Tastes
- Invasion of Your Home
- Gifts
- Computer Use
- Cell Phones and Pagers
- Physical Evidence
- His Behavior Around Other Women
- Accidental Slip-ups or Disclosures

In addition to documenting well over 800 telltale signs, *Is He Cheating On You?* also tells you how to evaluate what you find and gives you a starting point for figuring out what to do next.

NOTE: This book is written specifically for women who suspect their husbands of cheating on them. But many of the signs are universal and apply to cheating wives as well.

Chapter 2

WHY BOTHER TO FIND OUT?

Should you investigate your husband if you suspect him of cheating on you? Why even bother trying find out? Why go to all this trouble to discover something you'd probably rather not know? Why not take the course of least resistance and leave things as they are? Why not just look the other way until his cheating becomes too blatant to ignore or until someone brings it to your attention? Why not just pretend it's not happening and hope for the best?

Ignorance is Not Bliss

Despite what others may tell you, ignorance is *not* bliss. Ignoring your husband's affair will not make it go away. Experts say that if a woman does not find out about her husband's cheating, he's likely to continue. If your husband is cheating, ignoring his behavior could cause the situation to become a permanent state of affairs. Turning a blind eye can cause irreparable harm to your marriage. By pretending it's not happening, you create a permissive environment. The longer you pretend not to know, the more likely he is to continue, because he thinks he's getting away with it or feels he has your silent approval.

Ignoring things will not make them better In fact, things could get progressively worse. Your husband could become so attached to his lover that it will be difficult for him to give her up and get your marriage back on track. Sure, you could passively sit back and wait for your husband to tire of his lover. But what if he gets tired of *you* instead and decide to leave you for her?

Your Future is at Stake

No doubt you've heard stories of husbands who abandon their wives after years of marriage. What if your husband leaves you and you've done nothing to prepare yourself financially or emotionally for this traumatic change of events? The sooner you find out what you're up against, the sooner you can take action. You owe it to yourself—and your children, if you have any— to ferret out the truth. *"Is he cheating on me?"* Once that question takes root in your mind, it can haunt you day and night. It will create anxieties that spill over into other areas of your life. This, in turn, will affect the way you react toward friends, family and the world around you. It can manifest itself as anger, depression, anxiety and more Your mental, physical and emotional well-being are at stake. So ignore anyone who tells you that you're better off not knowing the truth.

Why It Pays to Find Out the Truth

If you think your husband is cheating, it's in your best interest to find out if what you suspect is true. Here are twenty compelling reasons why:

1. **To put your mind at ease.** A strong suspicion that your husband may be cheating can cause you endless days of worry and many sleepless nights. If it turns out that he's *not* cheating, it will be a big relief to know your suspicions were untrue. The sooner you confront your suspicions, the sooner you can stop worrying and get on with your life.

2. **To take steps to protect yourself (and your children) financially.** Affairs cost money. Your husband may be tapping into the family's financial resources to maintain his affair. If you find evidence of this, you can take steps now to secure your (and your children's) financial well-being before he squanders more of the marital assets on his mistress. If he's paying for flowers, jewelry, gifts, dinners and hotel rooms with your joint credit cards, you could end up footing the bill for his affair.

3. **To eliminate the possibility of contracting HIV/AIDS or some other sexually transmitted disease.** HIV/AIDS and other STDs are a stark reality of life. If your husband is engaging in unprotected sex with another woman it can have life-threatening consequences—for you, him, or your unborn children. If you find out this type of reckless behavior is going on behind your back, you can take steps to protect yourself.

4. **To prepare yourself emotionally for the possibility that your husband may leave you.** If your husband's involvement with his lover becomes so strong that he decides to leave you for her, wouldn't you rather know in advance? The last thing you want is to have him spring it on you by surprise. As devastating as it may be, knowing that this is a possibility gives you time to mentally and emotionally adjust to the idea.

5. **To keep unfounded suspicions from poisoning your marriage and your mind.** No matter how carefully you conceal what you suspect, if you think your husband is cheating, these thoughts will poison your mind. You'll view him in a different light. This will eventually affect various aspects of your marriage — your sex life, your daily interaction with your husband, the level of trust you have. If your suspicions turn out to be false, confirming this can restore the balance and breathe new life into your marriage.

6. **To seek legal counsel and find out your rights.** You'll want to arm yourself legally if you suspect your husband of having an affair. Avail yourself of a free (or low-cost) consultation with an attorney who specializes in matrimonial law. Find out as soon as possible what your legal rights are (alimony, child support, division of marital assets, etc.), even if you're not sure at this point what you will do. Whether you decide to dissolve your marriage or stay with your husband and try to work things out, you need to have this information.

7. To gather evidence so you can confront your husband with your knowledge of his affair. Often the key attraction of an affair is the secrecy, the intrigue, the sense of getting away with something forbidden. For many men, once the affair is out in the open, it loses its appeal. Experts all agree that if you've found concrete evidence that your husband is cheating, you should confront him with your knowledge of his affair. Many times, this in itself will bring the situation to a halt.

8. To short-circuit an affair in the making. Affairs usually happen in stages Most men don't become cheating husbands overnight. Your husband may not have actually cheated on you yet, but he could be seriously entertaining "pre-infidelity thoughts." Detecting the early warning signs of an impending affair will give you a chance to stop things before they begin.

9. To seek professional help in coping with your husband's affair. A skilled marriage counselor or family therapist can help you work through the emotional trauma that accompanies the discovery of an affair. He or she can guide you through the aftermath of the affair and work with you individually or as a couple to get your marriage back on track and avoid an unnecessary divorce. If divorce is inevitable, your counselor or therapist can help you rebuild your life.

10. To gain control of the situation. You can feel like a helpless victim if you're not sure what's going on. And you can easily get swept along with the tide. Knowledge is power. Once you find out the facts, the ball is in your court. You can take control of the situation by making an informed decision about how to handle the matter. You may even be able to turn things around to your advantage.

11. To find out exactly what you're dealing with. Lately your husband has been acting strangely. Maybe he's cheating on you. But what if there's another reason for his strange behavior? If there's some other problem or issue that's threatening the stability of your marriage, you need to know. Some discreet detective work on your part will help you find out what's really going on.

12. **To safeguard your financial assets if your husband is planning to leave you.** What about your financial security? An unexpected divorce or separation can put an unsuspecting wife in a serious financial bind. Consider the financial implications of your situation (living arrangements, child care, transportation, bills etc.) if your husband leaves you high and dry. Don't automatically assume he'll continue to provide for you and the children after he's gone. Cheating husbands who plan to leave their wives often transfer ownership, liquidate, divert or otherwise conceal marital assets and resources. What if he remarries? If you know in advance that your husband is cheating, you can take steps to prepare for these possibilities. There maybe certain things you need to do now to maintain your financial status quo.

13. **To gain the time you need to fight for your marriage.** If you know your husband is seeing someone else, you can examine yourself and your marriage to see what may have triggered the affair. If you can pinpoint the contributing factors, you have a fighting chance to make changes that can save your marriage from divorce.

14. **To determine whether your marriage is in jeopardy.** All affairs are not the same. Some affairs pose more of a threat to a relationship than others. Things may not be as bad as you think – or they could be a whole lot worse. A little detective work will help you determine whether your husband is having a frivolous "fling;" or whether he's forged a deep emotional bond that will be difficult to break.

15. **To focus your energy in the right direction.** You can waste endless time and energy wondering: *"Is he? Isn't he?"* You'll be in a constant state of emotional limbo until you find out what's going on. Taking matters into your own hands is not only therapeutic, it will help you get to the bottom of things. Once you have a clear

picture of the situation, you can figure out what to do. If he is cheating, you can focus your energy on planning how to handle the situation.

16. **To get the facts out into the open, so together, the two of you can work to get your marriage back on track.** Sometimes an affair can serve as a wake-up call for a marriage. If you find out for sure that your husband is cheating, the two of you (alone or with the help of a marriage counselor) can pinpoint and address the underlying problems in your marriage which may have contributed to his affair. Dealing with the root of the problem can lessen the likelihood of your husband straying again.

17. **To obtain court-admissible proof of his cheating in preparation for taking legal action (divorce or child custody).** If you decide to sue for divorce or child custody, you'll need proof of your husband's infidelity that will hold up in a court of law. Once you establish that he is, in fact cheating on you, it makes sense to hire an investigator to obtain whatever legal proof you may need.(If you've done much of the preliminary footwork, your bill should be considerably lower.)

18. **To make rational decisions about your future based on facts rather than assumptions.** If your suspicions about your husband haven't been confirmed, don't take action of any kind until you're absolutely sure. It would be foolish to leave your husband, put him out, or start divorce proceedings on the basis of speculation about what *might* be going on. Don't speculate – investigate. Get the facts, then proceed. Base your decision on reliable information.

19. **To put an end to malicious rumors and gossip.** It's embarrassing and humiliating to be grist for the rumor mill. Others might also suspect your husband of cheating on you, but things may not be what they seem. There could be a valid explanation for your husband's behavior. If your investigation reveals that he's not cheating, you can silence those wagging tongues.

Malicious gossip, lies and rumors will roll off you like the proverbial water off a duck's back.

20. **To punish the scoundrel or seek revenge.** (*not really a good idea*) I don't recommend this at all, but many women feel justified in exacting revenge or punishing their husbands for being unfaithful to them. I strongly discourage you from doing this. A desire for revenge can be a recipe for disaster. Getting revenge may make you feel better for the moment, but in the long run, it's not worth the time and effort. The newspapers and prison systems are full of women who overstepped the boundaries of the law to get revenge on a cheating husband.

Whatever your personal reasons are for wanting to find out if your husband is cheating on you, this book will help you discover the truth.

Don't speculate – investigate!

Chapter 3

THE TELLTALE SIGNS ARE THERE

Trust me, if your husband is cheating on you, the telltale signs are there—even if you can't recognize them yet. Though he may take pains to avoid leaving obvious clues, a cheating man will reveal himself with signs so subtle it wouldn't occur to him to cover them up. Not all cheating husbands act the same, but there's one thing they all have in common: to cheat on his wife, he has to make changes in one or more aspects of his life in order to accommodate his affair. Those changes are telltale signs.

Changes Will Give Him Away
If he's cheating, your husband will want to look (and smell) his best for his lover. Hence he'll pay more than the usual attention to his physical appearance. There will be easily detectable changes in his wardrobe, weight, hairstyle, dental hygiene, or grooming routine.

He must communicate with his lover. He has to stay in touch with her whether by telephone, cell phone, e-mail, pager, letter or in person. Unless it's a one-night stand, he has to meet her somewhere, with some degree of regularity—whether it's weekly, bi-monthly or some other arrangement. He usually has to spend money on her – dinner, entertainment, hotels, gifts, flowers or vacations. And he has to figure out how to do all this without arousing suspicion or getting caught.

The key thing to look for is **change.** It's almost impossible for a man to cheat without changing something about himself, his lifestyle or his daily routine. In many cases, he'll be totally unaware of the changes in himself and his routine – one reason certain signs can't be easily concealed. Some of the changes are so minor he'd never even think to cover them up. His mind will be preoccupied, his speech guarded. His stress, obsession or excitement over all this will affect the way he relates to you and everyone around him. He may become so caught up in the excitement of his affair that he throws ordinary caution to the winds or just plain forgets to cover his tracks.

Spotting the Signs

There are well over 800 telltale signs listed in this book. Since no two men are alike, no two cheating husbands will display exactly the same telltale signs. Nor will any man display every sign listed in this book. Some telltale signs are easy to spot. Some changes are so radical, they'll be impossible to ignore. Others changes require close observation to detect. But knowing what to look for will enable you to easily recognize most of the telltale signs.

Many telltale signs are negative. Your husband may become ill-tempered, impatient, belligerent or begin criticizing everything you say or do. He may snap at you, become verbally or physically abusive or completely ignore you.

On the other hand, some telltale signs are quite positive. Your husband may suddenly become very generous and shower you with gifts. He may become more cheerful, more passionate, more attentive or easier to get along with. He may even display a newfound zest for life.

Since you know your marriage better than anyone else, you're the best judge of what constitutes unusual behavior for your husband. If you make a point of staying tuned in to his behavior, you'll spot any departures from his norm. If you're extremely observant, you might even be able to determine the identity of the "other woman."

Chapter 4

HOW TO FIND
THE TELLTALE SIGNS

The telltale signs are grouped into 21 categories so you can easily locate the signs that apply to your husband. Look through the signs, then give yourself a reasonable period of time (3 to 6 weeks) to search for clues. Watch your husband. Pay close attention to everything he says or does. While it's true that some telltale signs are subtle, most are easy to spot, when you know what you're looking for. If you stay alert to what's going on, you're unlikely to miss any significant signs.

- **Look** – at his appearance, notice his behavior. Observe the changes in his work habits and his daily routine.

- **Listen** – for uncharacteristic remarks, for things he now refuses to discuss, for names dropped, for lies or inconsistencies in what he says.

- **Smell** – his person, his clothing, his car for incriminating sexual odors or unfamiliar scents.

- **Feel** – the tension in your marriage, the emotional distance.

Don't be so quick to dismiss your intuition. If your gut instinct tells you something is wrong, take a closer look.

Stay Alert

Don't let a single day pass without being keenly aware of everything your husband says or does. The signs that are evident one day may be undetectable the next. Be alert to anything that appears to be a departure from his norm.

Some women make a point of actively searching for telltale signs. Others feel so strongly about invasion of privacy that they only take notice of readily visible telltale signs. To them, certain boundaries are not to be crossed, even for a worthy cause. If you feel uneasy about spying on your husband, do what feels comfortable to you. It helps to think of it as information gathering rather than spying. Bear in mind that sometimes the end justifies the means. The more diligently you search, the more signs you're likely to find. Some women observe telltale signs but don't recognize them for what they are. They make no connection between what they see and what's going on behind their back. You won't miss much if you constantly refer to the categories in this book.

Write Down What You Find

Document everything! Keep accurate records of what you find. Don't try to rely on your memory. Record your findings in a journal and keep it under lock and key. Log in the dates, times and places that suspicious incidents occur (phone calls, absences, meetings, excuses or alibis given, names mentioned, etc.). With everything down in black-and-white, you can analyze what you've found to see if there are patterns to his behavior. Does he have to go to the store for cigarettes or a beer around 8:30 every Thursday night? Do anonymous phone calls only come a half hour before (or after) he leaves for his weekly night out with the guys? Does he walk the dog an unusually long time the first and third Sunday of each month? Does he put on cologne to go work out at the gym? Does he wear his best suit or one of his favorite shirts only when he has to work late? Patterns like these will only be evident if you carefully document the things you find.

Exercise Caution

When you find tangible, physical evidence, pay close attention to exactly where and how it was found. Be careful to put things back exactly as they were to keep from arousing his suspicion. When possible, make photocopies or take photos of love notes, phone numbers, e-mails, letters, incriminating receipts and similar items you happen to come across. Store your "evidence journal" in a safe place. You'll need it when you sit down and tell your husband you know his affair.

As you go about conducting your investigation, *be discreet.* Keep your eyes and ears open and your mouth shut. Maintain your secrecy; be careful not to tip your hand. Don't let your husband know that you suspect anything at all. Live your life as normally as you can while checking your husband out. Treat him the same way you did before you began to have doubts. If you don't, he may become suspicious. Once he gets wind that you're "on to him", he may start hiding evidence or attempt to cover his tracks. As long as he doesn't know that you're suspicious, it will be easier to find out what's going on.

Don't Ask – He Won't Tell

Keep watching your husband and the pieces of the puzzle will slowly start falling into place. A lot of his strange behavior will suddenly begin to make sense. However, you should prepare yourself for the possibility that it could take weeks for you to find out the truth. During the time you're observing your husband, you may be tempted to question him about some of the things you see or hear. You'll feel an overwhelming urge to drop a few hints about what you've found just to let him know you're not a fool. My advice to you is *don't*. If you give in to these urges prematurely, you'll be making a serious mistake. Keep your lips zipped and your emotions in check until you have all the facts. Timing is everything. Don't lose the advantage you have by exposing your knowledge too soon.

Restrain Yourself

It will take great effort on your part to restrain yourself as the evidence against your husband mounts. *Do not* come right out and ask him if he's having an affair unless you've prepared yourself to hear a lie. It usually takes solid evidence before a cheating husband will reluctantly (if ever) admit to having an affair. Even then, many men continue to lie. Ask a few discreet questions, if you must, but refrain from giving him the third degree.

Continue your search for telltale signs and put your major questions on hold. Jot them down in a special section of your evidence journal. You'll get a chance to ask them later when you sit down and talk with him about his affair. Restrain yourself for now. There's nothing to be gained by dropping hints or letting your husband know what you suspect. Reveal your knowledge only at the right time, under the right circumstances.

The more information you gather about your husband's affair, the more fragile your emotions may become — or the hotter your anger will begin to blaze. If the pain of discovery becomes unbearable or you become too filled with rage to continue, hire a professional who can investigate from an impersonal point of view.

Build a Strong Case

Once you have solid evidence that your husband is cheating, experts agree that you should confront him with your knowledge of his affair. Make sure your case is strong and your evidence solid. It will be hard for him to deny the truth if you have it down in black and white. That's why it's so important that you keep accurate notes. He may try to confuse you or convince you it's all in your mind. This is a common ploy of cheating husbands when confronted with evidence of their affair.

Plan Your Confrontation

When the time is right for you to confront your husband with what you know about his affair, the time, place and goals of your confrontation must be carefully planned. When you confront him, there are specific questions you'll need to ask him about the affair. For more detailed information, get a copy of **"How to Confront your Husband about His Affair."** It will coach you on how to proceed for the best results.

A WORD OF CAUTION

Do not jeopardize your safety searching for telltale signs. Take all necessary precautions to protect yourself and your children. If at any time you feel that you are in danger; or if your husband has aggressive tendencies, an explosive temper or has a history of violent behavior, leave the detective work to a pro. ***Do not put yourself or your children at risk.***

Chapter 5

WHEN SHOULD YOU HIRE
A DETECTIVE?

Many women feel they should hire a private investigator right from the start, despite the fact that there are telltale signs they can easily discover for themselves. However, bear in mind that there are numerous signs an investigator is unlikely to find without your help. As you'll see, if you flip through the categories of telltale signs in this book, many are things that only a wife is in a position to know. My personal recommendation is to first do a little digging on your own. Then if your preliminary search warrants it, and you don't mind spending the money, hire a professional to do the rest. The more basic information you provide your investigator with, the more quickly and efficiently he can work - and the lower your final cost will be.

Look for a detective who specializes in infidelity, spousal, matrimonial, or domestic investigations, as they're sometimes called. They can obtain names, addresses, photos, videotapes, and other types of documentation, if you need proof in order to take legal action. However, sometimes there are circumstances when it's advisable to hire an investigator right from the start.

Is It Intuition or Insecurity?

According to statistics, 85% of women who had a "gut feeling" that their husbands were cheating turned out to be right. But let me issue a word of caution here: Don't confuse intuition with insecurity. No matter how strong your suspicion may be, don't accuse your husband of cheating, unless you have solid proof. Before you confront your husband about having an affair, make sure you're on solid ground. Your suspicions could turn out to be totally groundless if you:

- are suspicious by nature
- have a natural distrust of men
- have issues with jealousy
- are emotionally insecure
- suffer from low self-esteem
- are paranoid
- have an overly active imagination

If any of the above apply to you, my advice is to hire a detective. Under the above circumstances, you're not the best person to check your husband out. What you need is a professional who will conduct a fair and impartial investigation, and provide you with documented proof of your husband's innocence or guilt.

Chapter 6

PREPARE YOURSELF BEFOREHAND
FOR WHAT YOU MIGHT FIND

Have you given any serious thought as to what you'll do if it turns out your husband really is cheating? Before you set out on your search for telltale signs, you should prepare yourself mentally and emotionally for what you might find. If you're like most women, you don't have a game plan in place for dealing with infidelity. It's probably one of those things you never expected to happen to you. Of course you're hoping for the best, but it's wise to prepare yourself for the worst.

What Will You Do?

If your investigation reveals that your husband is cheating on you, how will you handle the situation? Stop and give the matter some serious thought. Who will you turn to for help? Will you leave your husband? Will you put him out? Will you end your marriage or stay with your husband and try to work things out? While you are still able to think clearly and objectively, mentally explore some of the possible options you could take. What would it be in your (and your children's) best interest to do? Analyze the situation now and map out a possible plan of action.

Three Essential People

Most women, when suddenly confronted with infidelity in their marriage. have no idea what to do or who to turn to for help. They let anger, panic, fear or jealousy cause them to do things they later regret. Before going any further, you need to put a support system in place. It should consist of the first three of the following people :

- a confidante
- an attorney well-versed in family law
- a marriage/family counselor or relationship therapist
- a private investigator (optional)

These individuals will be essential to your emotional and physical well-being should you find that you are indeed a victim of infidelity. Find, choose or get referrals for each member of your personal support team now. When the time comes that you actually need them, you'll be too devastated to make wise choices then. Remember the Girl Scout motto: "Be prepared." Let's see what will be required from each one.

Confidante

You will need someone you can trust to confide in – a caring, sympathetic *female* friend — a family member or a girlfriend. Notice that I stress that your confidante should be *female*. It's best not to choose a male for this role. (The rare exception might be a brother, uncle or close relative.) Confiding in a male at such a vulnerable point in your life will only invite more trouble. If your husband is cheating, you've already got trouble enough. The ideal choice would be a woman who is an infidelity survivor herself.

Choose your confidante wisely. Be extremely careful about who you take into your confience. Make absolutely sure there's no possible chance that the female friend you choose could be "the other woman." Don't take this advice lightly. I can't emphasize this strongly enough. It's not uncommon for a man to have an affair with an in-law, a neighbor, a family friend or even his wife's best friend. Find a female you can trust — someone you can pour your heart out to. Someone compassionate who will listen patiently and sympathetically without criticizing or telling you what to do.

Attorney

Get several recommendations and locate an attorney who specializes in matrimonial law. If you can't get a referral from someone you trust, try to find an attorney who is a member of the American Academy of Matrimonial Lawyers (www.aaml.org). Whether you ultimately decide to stay with your husband or not, you need someone knowledgeable who can advise you of your rights. You need to fully understand the legal implications of your situation. Consulting an attorney does not mean that you are starting or even considering divorce proceedings. All you want at this point is to be aware of your options with respect to child support, alimony, distribution of marital assets, living arrangements, financial obligations and other legal matters. Many attorneys offer free or low-cost initial consultations. When you call for an appointment, inquire about the fee. You may even be able to get basic information over the phone.

Marriage Counselor or Relationship Therapist:

You'll also need the help of a good marriage/family counselor or relationship therapist. Get several recommendations and choose one well ahead of time. Ideally the therapist you choose should be a member of The American Association for Marriage and Family Therapy. To find one near you visit their web site (www.TherapistLocator.net). Women frequently need professional help to deal with the emotional trauma associated with the discovery of their husband's affair. If your husband refuses to admit or discuss his affair with you, a trained professional may be able to draw him out. You'll need to know certain things about your husband's affair before you make a decision about what to do. A skilled therapist can also help you put the affair in perspective, explore underlying marital problems, get your marriage back on track and avoid an unnecessary divorce. If divorce turns out to be the only solution, a therapist or counselor can help you work through the recovery stage.

Private Investigator

You may also want to consider adding a private investigator as the fourth member of your personal support team. Things may reach a point where you require a more detailed or more objective investigation than you're capable of conducting on your own. Look in the Yellow Pages or surf the Net for an investigator who specializes in domestic, matrimonial, spousal or infidelity investigations.

Make Sure You Do This First

Put your personal support team in place well in advance. Do not skip this step or put it off. Later, you may be too paralyzed with pain to make decisions with your best interests in mind. Once you've taken care of this, you're ready to start searching for telltale signs.

PART II

THE
TELLTALE SIGNS

Chapter 7

PHYSICAL APPEARANCE

A man having an affair (or even thinking about having one) will want to make himself appear more attractive. He'll begin to enhance his appearance in some way. Be alert for changes in his wardrobe, his grooming, his body, and his personal hygiene. If he embarks on a drastic self-induced makeover, it's probably not for you. More than likely he's trying to attract or impress someone else.

1. He develops a keen interest in his personal appearance. He becomes fixated on or obsessed with how he looks.

2. He starts keeping a change of clothing at work, in the trunk of the car or someplace else.

3. He starts using hair color products to cover his gray hair.

4. He buys new clothing.

5. He seems overly concerned about his weight or his muscle tone.

6. He showers or bathes as soon as he comes in – possibly to remove incriminating odors.

7. He wears cologne more often.

8. He becomes very meticulous with his clothing and his grooming routine.

9. He buys a toupee or gets a hair weave or hair implants to cover his bald spot.

10. He suddenly decides to join a health club or a gym.

11. He will fast, go on a diet, or embark on a weight loss campaign of some kind.

12. He quickly changes clothes when he comes home — possibly to conceal make-up stains, perfume or incriminating odors.

13. He changes his style of underwear — cotton BVD's are replaced by silk boxer shorts.

14. He drastically upgrades the quality of his clothing – going almost overnight from K-mart to Armani.

15. You start noticing expensive items of jewelry or clothing (probably gifts from her) that he tries to pass off as things he bought for himself.

16. He now trims his toenails regularly – without even being asked.

17. He hires a personal trainer.

18. He buys different (or more expensive) brands of shampoo, deodorant or other toiletries and grooming aids.

19. He takes his clothes to the dry cleaners more frequently; his dry cleaning bills increase.

20. Now he showers *every* night before coming to bed.

21. His wardrobe undergoes a radical change in style — from polished and professional to more casual and relaxed or from shabby to snazzy.

22. He's never without breath mints or gum to keep his breath fresh, or ChapStick to keep his lips soft and kissable. You find them all over the place–in his pockets, his dresser drawers, his car, his office, his briefcase or backpack.

23. He starts getting facials or manicures.

24. He comes home wearing different clothing than what he had on when he left.

25. He changes his hairstyle – long hair suddenly becomes short, short hair is allowed to grow long or he sports a new designer haircut.

26. He suddenly adopts a vigorous new fitness program — going almost overnight from couch potato to fitness fanatic.

27. He shines his shoes more often.

28. He displays undue anxiety about his clothes. He worries obsessively about whether or not he's appropriately dressed.

29. He increases the amount of cologne he wears.

30. He makes a point of dressing up to run errands or to hang out with the guys when he'd normally wear whatever he happened to have on.

31. He spends an excessive amount of time in front of the mirror primping or preening.

32. He always wears his best outfit or his favorite articles of clothing on certain days of the week or on the days he has to work late.

33. He starts sending his shirts out to the laundry or begins laundering or ironing them himself. (He could be trying to hide make-up stains.)

34. He takes longer or more frequent baths or showers.

35. He exhibits a newfound concern for style and fashion.

36. He shaves off his moustache — or grows one.

37. He makes a major investment in exercise equipment or fitness gadgets.

38. He switches from glasses to contact lenses.

39. He becomes obsessed with his dental hygiene, making a series of dental appointments for fillings, caps, cleaning, whitening, replacement of missing teeth or other dental work.

40. He switches from plain white underwear to colors or patterns.

41. He starts doing his own personal laundry.

42. He stops wearing sneakers everywhere he goes.

43. He switches to a different type of cologne from what he normally wears.

44. He graduates from store-bought to tailor-made suits.

45. Various articles of clothing repeatedly turn up missing. He claims to have thrown them away, donated them to charity or loaned them to a friend. (He could be keeping a change of clothes somewhere or trying to conceal lipstick or perfume).

46. He stops wearing his wedding band.

47. He goes on a health food kick.

48. He changes the colors or patterns he normally wears – from subdued and tasteful to bright loud or flashy. Or vice versa – from loud and flamboyant to conservative patterns or shades.

49. He now spends time poring over men's fashion magazines (GQ, Esquire, etc.).

50. He shaves off his beard – or decides to grow one.

51. He shampoos his hair more often.

52. He flosses or brushes his teeth more frequently.

53. He takes special care with his grooming (extra-close shave, wears cologne) on a specific day of the week or on days when he has to "work late."

54. He bathes or showers at unusual times or at times that he never did before.

55. He buys a new style of eyeglasses.

56. He starts jogging or biking to lose weight or improve his physique.

57. Instead of leaving his clothes lying around as usual, he immediately puts them away without being asked.

58. He starts combing his hair over his bald spot.

59. He spends an excessive amount of money buying new or additional toiletries or grooming aids.

60. You catch him using your toiletries (shampoo, facial cream, body lotion).

61. Your formerly "Sloppy Joe" is now always impeccably dressed.

62. He starts lifting weights.

63. He starts going to a tanning salon.

64. He plucks the gray hairs from his moustache or beard.

65. He comes home with his clothing looking rumpled, disheveled, wrinkled, inside out or backwards.

66. He gives extra attention to his grooming – it now takes him twice as long to get dressed.

66. He now uses mouthwash regularly and always has minty fresh breath.

68. He starts spraying his clothing with an odor neutralizer (like Febreze) to get rid of incriminating smells.

69. He no longer wants you to buy his clothing. Now he wants to shop for himself.

70. He's overly concerned about how his clothing fits. He may run up a large tailoring or alteration bill.

71. He starts doing sit-ups, crunches or push-ups every day.

72. He buys shoes with lifts in them to enhance his height.

73. He removes his wedding band when he's getting a tan, so there's no telltale tan line on his finger when he takes off his ring to cheat.

74. He returns home from a "night out with the guys" minus items of clothing or jewelry (socks, tie, jacket, watch, ring, etc)

75. You find lipstick smudges on his collar, sleeve, the front of his shirt or jacket or on his body.

76. He changes his hair color.

Chapter 8

HOW HE RELATES TO YOU

The way your husband relates to you can provide many telltale signs. His involvement with another woman will cause him to treat you differently even on an unconscious level. This is one of the areas where a wife can pick up telltale signs that an investigator might otherwise overlook.

1. He's less attentive towards you.

2. He's rude and disrespectful to you.

3. He no longer wants to do fun things together. (He's having his fun with someone else.)

4. He starts showering you with gifts or buying you flowers for no special reason. (He's motivated by guilt).

5. He doesn't make eye contact with you anymore – his guilt won't let him look you in the eye.

6. He's now overly affectionate with you in public or at social functions. (He's putting on an act to convince the world that everything between you is okay.)

7. He develops an abnormal interest in your schedule. He

wants to know where you're going, how long you'll be there and what time you're coming back.

8. He picks fights with you over trivial things so he can have an excuse to storm out of the house, "go for a drive" or "take a walk" to calm down.

9. He no longer wants to spend time alone with you. He always wants other people around (friends, relatives, the kids). Even when you go out together, he wants to bring another couple along.

10. He becomes inconsiderate of your feelings or begins to mistreat you in little ways.

11. He seems angry with you all the time.

12. He accuses you of checking up on him.

13. He starts acting very formal or overly polite toward you.

14. He becomes highly critical of you. He finds fault with everything you say or do—the way you dress, look, speak, act, keep house, cook—nothing you do is right.

15. Your presence seems to annoy him.

16. He begins to distance himself from you emotionally – because of guilt, uncertainty, or internal conflict.

17. He seems to be avoiding you. When you enter a room, he gets up and leaves.

18. He stops being romantic.

19. He becomes very attentive or unusually considerate toward you. Suddenly he's just being too darn nice.

20. He complains to friends and family (yours or his) about you.

21. He suddenly becomes more complimentary towards you.

22. He stops giving you compliments.

23. If you attempt to hold his hand, he pulls away.

24. He doesn't laugh at your jokes anymore.

25. He no longer seems interested in you or the marriage.

26. He acts guilty when you do something nice for him.

27. He encourages you to spend more time with your friends or family.

28. He no longer notices when you get your hair or nails done or wear a new outfit.

29. He doesn't want to go anywhere or do anything with you any more. He refuses to take part in activities that the two of you once enjoyed together.

30. He rejects offers of affection from you – pulls away when you try to hug him, turns his face aside when you attempt to kiss him.

31. He "throws cold water" on your efforts to engage him in conversation.

32. He's impatient with you.

33. He insists he told you something that you know he never mentioned – forgetting that he told her instead.

34. He accuses you of being jealous or not trusting him.

35. He no longer shows any interest in you and the things that are going on in your life.

36. He starts encouraging you to get involved in private pursuits (graduate school, adult education classes, a part-time job, volunteer work, business venture) all activities that will occupy a significant amount of your time. (You'll be too busy to keep up with what he's doing.)

37. He starts accusing *you* of cheating on *him*, to put you on the defensive and deflect suspicion away from himself.

38. He refuses to accompany you to family events. (reunions, holiday or social gatherings, weddings, funerals, graduations, etc.)

39. He feels the two of you should remain married but start leading separate lives. (He wants to have his cake and eat it too!)

40. There's a tension between the two of you that you can't quite put your finger on.

41. He no longer wants to spend quality time with you.

43. He calls you at work to find out what time you're coming home or what your plans are after work. (He's trying to set up a rendezvous with his lover.)

44. He's created his own little world – and it doesn't include you.

45. He becomes stubborn and uncooperative.

46. He becomes physically abusive.

47. He's no longer as supportive as he once was.

48. He encourages you to go shopping, knowing this will give him a large block of free time.

49. He starts questioning your love for him.

50. He constantly picks fights with you.

51. You sense an unexplainable distance between you that wasn't there before.

52. He's indifferent to issues that would normally concern the two of you.

53. You catch him staring at you with a look of annoyance or disdain.

54. If he spends quality time with you, he does so begrudgingly.

55. He tries to convince you your suspicions of him are "all in your mind" or just a "figment of your imagination."

56. He calls to verify that you're still where you said you'd be so he won't get caught by surprise.

57. When he engages in his favorite activities (fishing, skiing, hiking, museum hopping, watching videos, etc.) he no longer wants you around.

58. He seems aloof, emotionally detached or preoccupied.

59. He keeps encouraging you to have a night out with the girls or spend more time with your friends.

60. He suggests you take a lover. (So he can justify his affair or lessen his guilt.)

61. He speaks harshly to you.

62. He no longer cares where you go or what you do.

63. If you ask to accompany him when he's going out, he either gets angry, refuses to take you, changes his destination or decides to stay home.

64. He busies himself with hobbies, TV, surfing the Net — anything to avoid interacting with you.

65. He becomes sullen and resentful if you ask him to do something for you.

66. He goes out of his way to avoid physical closeness – moves over if you sit next to him, pushes you away if you attempt to sit on his lap, shrugs off your hand if you touch him.

67. Lately he's always comparing you (unfavorably) to someone else – a particular female friend, coworker or neighbor.

68. He never has anything nice to say to you or about you anymore.

69. He's reluctant to make or commit to any long-range plans that involve you.

70. He won't take baths or showers with you anymore.

Chapter 9

CONVERSATIONAL CLUES

What your husband chooses or refuses to talk about can alert you to his involvement in an extramarital affair. Even his tone of voice can be a telltale sign.

1. He no longer shares the events of his day with you.

2. He starts using words, phrases or slang expressions that you've never heard him use before.

3. He stops asking you about the personal things that are going on in your life.

4. He stops communicating at home and has little or nothing to say. (Men often clam up when they're cheating for fear they'll let something slip.)

5. When he addresses you, he no longer uses terms of endearment like "baby/babe," "honey," "sweetheart" or "dear."

6. He doesn't say "I love you" anymore.

7. Overnight he starts speaking authoritatively about subjects of which he previously had no knowledge.

8. He talks about taking separate vacations.

9. You sense that he's tuning you out when you talk.

10. He talks incessantly about a particular female (coworker, neighbor, or acquaintance) making constant reference to her ideas, her opinions, her insightful remarks, her problems, her personal habits, her likes and dislikes and other details about her life. If a particular female becomes his main topic of conversation, it behooves you to check her out.

11. He speaks very harshly or rudely to you.

12. When he talks with you, he avoids looking you in the eye.

13. He becomes verbally abusive – cursing, belittling or ridiculing you whether you're alone or in the presence of others.

14. He talks about needing space or time alone.

15. He casually mentions getting a weekend place so he can get away on his own.

16. Communication between the two of you reaches an all time low. Talking with him is like pulling teeth. He makes you feel like you're conducting an interrogation instead of carrying on a conversation.

17. He starts spouting ideas and opinions that are clearly not his own.

18. His conversation becomes very superficial. He no longer discusses confidential matters or shares his innermost feelings and thoughts with you.

19. He has frequent or lengthy phone conversations with a female "friend."

20. He absorbs himself in TV, hobbies, surfing the Net or doing personal projects to avoid conversation with you.

21. He gives you detailed and lengthy explanations for his absences, when he never used to account for his time before.

22. He becomes defensive during normal conversations.

23. The names of friends that he talked about on a regular basis suddenly disappear from his conversation. (If it's a male friend, he may be covering up for your husband. If it's a female, she could be his lover.)

24. He no longer engages in pillow talk after you make love.

25. He stops using his pet name(s) for you.

26. He starts reminiscing about the single life or speculating about what it would be like to be a single man again.

27. He refers to a movie or play that you haven't seen—forgetting he saw it with her instead of you.

28. He accuses you of being jealous.

29. He makes insulting or disrespectful remarks to you or about you when you're in public.

30. He starts sharing intimate details of his life with a female who's supposedly just a "friend."

31. When the two of you are with others, he excludes you from the conversation.

32. He asks you all kinds of personal questions about one of your female friends, relatives or coworkers.

33. He starts dropping new names into the conversation.

34. Conversation between the two of you has become awkward or strained.

35. He becomes more talkative.

36. He alludes to or talks openly about separation or divorce. (He's probably got a lover waiting in the wings.)

37. He makes derogatory remarks to his male friends about you.

38. He regularly discusses your marital problems with a female friend of yours (or his).

39. He no longer talks about what he does with his time when he's away from you.

40. He hints that he's seeing or is interested in someone else.

41. If you try to start a conversation with him he answers you abruptly or brushes you off.

42. He starts criticizing and complaining about everything you say or do.

43. He starts talking about how unhappy, bored or dissatisfied he is with his life.

44. He pointedly talks about getting together with old friends he hasn't seen in years. (It could be an alibi.)

45. He makes excessive reference to specific male friends by name, expounding at great length on the activities he plans to participate in with them. (He could be laying the groundwork for an alibi.)

46. He no longer engages in intimate conversations with you.

47. He belittles or makes fun of your opinions or ideas.

48. He evades any talk about the future and ignores any references you make to future events and plans together.

49. He accuses you of checking up on him.

50. He stutters, stumbles or trips over his words when you ask innocent questions.

51. He's offended by comments that wouldn't ordinarily upset him.

52. He accuses *you* of cheating on *him*.

53. He talks about how unhappy he is in the marriage.

54. He expresses dissatisfaction with his body, his weight or his physique as a prelude to getting in shape to impress his lover.

55. He suggests (or insists) that you wear your hair like, dress like or otherwise imitate a certain female.

56. He starts talking about "open marriage" or "swinging."

57. He gets defensive if you mention anything that has to do with infidelity, cheating or extramarital affairs.

58. He has the audacity to suggest that you should take a lover — so he can justify his affair.

59. When you ask him what's wrong, either he refuses to discuss it, pretends he doesn't know what you mean, or snaps "Nothing!"

60. He changes the subject when you try to talk to him about things that are important to you: your job, your health, your friends, your family.

61. He gives you the silent treatment – going for hours or days without speaking to you.

62. He's always comparing you unfavorably to someone else.

63. Things you say that he used to find funny, cute or endearing, now irritate or annoy him.

64. He makes frequent references to your marriage ending – "If we split up, the dog goes with me." Or "if we ever get divorced, I want the kids at least 2 weekends every month."

65. He tells you how much he enjoys talking to a particular female.

66. He accuses you of making demands on his time.

67. Whenever he tells you he has to work late, there's a certain enthusiasm in his voice, like he's actually looking forward to it.

68. He begins making disparaging remarks about a particular female. (Either to cover up his true feelings for her or to discourage you from talking to her because she knows about his affair.)

69. He answers in monosyllables when you try to engage him in conversation.

70. He's always talking about how much he and a certain female have in common or tells you how well she understands him.

Chapter 10

WORK HABITS

Work is a common excuse to account for large blocks of time away. Men often use their jobs to cover up their extramarital affairs. Your husband's work habits will undoubtedly change as his affair unfolds. Be on the lookout for any of the telltale signs below.

1. You call his job to speak to him and find out he took the day off.

2. He says he's working late at the office, but no one answers the phone when you call.

3. He doesn't tell you the location of the "late meeting" he has to attend.

4. The smell of perfume, sex or alcohol accompanies him when he comes in late from "work."

5. There's a sudden increase in the number of business trips he has to take.

6. You find out his boss has no knowledge of the overtime or the extra days your husband claims he's been working.

7. He now leaves for work much earlier (so he can meet his lover for a pre-work rendezvous).

8. He now has to work on holidays.

9. He stops inviting you to office parties, company picnics and other social events for employees and their spouses.

10. You drop by his job unexpectedly and everyone seems to be nervous because you're there.

11. Lately he's been coming home much later than usual.

12. His cell phone always seems to malfunction (accidentally turned off, battery low, out of range) on the nights when he has to work late.

13. He claims he's working overtime, but his paycheck remains the same. (Check his paystub to confirm the number of hours he worked and the increase —or lack thereof— in pay.)

14. The name of one particular female on his job crops up repeatedly in his conversation.

15. A co-worker, his secretary, or a female employee acts too familiar around him.

16. He works late at times that are unusual for him. (He usually works on Monday nights, now it's Wednesday nights too. Or instead of one weekend a month, now it's every weekend).

17. He now has to "work" through his lunch hour and can no longer meet you for lunch.

18. He uses "new business associates" as an excuse for staying out late.

19. When you mention in the presence of his friends or coworkers that he's been working late, they act surprised or smug – as if they know it's not true.

20. At odd hours, he suddenly remembers something he forgot to do at work that requires him to return after normal business hours.

21. He tells you he's calling from the job, but the Caller ID says he's calling from someplace else.

22. He tells you he now has to entertain clients after work, when he never had to do so before.

23. He claims to be working overtime or doing extra work in the evenings or on weekends.

24. He starts keeping a shaver/razor and various toiletries or grooming aids at work.

25. His coworkers (or a specific female coworker) behave strangely around you or act nervous or uncomfortable in your presence.

26. At the end of the workday he suddenly discovers he has to work late.

27. When you call him at work, his secretary or coworkers have no idea where he is or have trouble tracking him down.

28. He takes unusually long lunch hours.

29. He and his secretary or coworkers have conflicting stories about why he's not at work when you call.

30. He lies about his salary – tells you he didn't get that raise or that annual bonus, but his paycheck indicates that he did.

31. Instead of getting a physical paycheck, he switches to direct deposit in a misguided attempt to conceal his income from you.

32. He removes the pictures of you and the children from his desk.

33. It's obvious that his secretary or a co-worker is trying to cover up for him when you call.

34. You drop by his job, he's not there, and no one knows where he is.

35. You hear about office functions that include spouses long after they've taken place.

36. He tells you spouses aren't invited to the company picnic or office Christmas party this year.

37. He doesn't want you to visit him at work.

38. He waits until the last minute to inform you about office parties, company picnics or other job functions that spouses can attend, so it's too late for you to accompany him.

39. He tells you he has a part time job. Is he really working? Or is it a cover-up for time spent with his lover?

Chapter 11

DAY-TO-DAY BEHAVIOR

We are all creatures of habit. All of us have a routine that we usually follow each day. A man who is cheating will display changes of some kind in his normal patterns of behavior. Pay close attention to deviations in your husband's daily routine. These deviations are telltale signs.

1. He develops a passion for things that never interested him before.

2. He's spending more time than usual at the gym. (Are you sure he's really working out? If so, with whom?)

3. He has new friends who he refuses to let you meet. (Either they're non-existent, or they're personal friends of hers.)

4. He stops checking in routinely with you during the day. Now you don't hear from him at all.

5. Instead of dragging himself out of bed each morning, he springs up full of energy, eager to start his day. (Affairs have a way of infusing men with new vitality.)

6. He makes a point of checking your whereabouts when you're at home so he can call his lover from another room.

7. He starts associating with men who are single, divorced, separated, or other men who are cheating on their wives or girlfriends. (Birds of a feather will flock together. Association brings on assimilation.)

8. He now undresses in the dark or in the bathroom—either he's overcome with a false sense of modesty because of his affair, or he has marks on his body that he doesn't want you to see.

9. He loses interest in the things that used to appeal to him – sports, hobbies, favorite pastimes etc.

10. Shirts, ties, underwear or other articles of clothing frequently turn up missing (They could be at her place.)

11. He uses words or expressions you've, never heard him use before.

12. He develops new outside interests - particularly ones that don't include you.

13. His usual household chores go undone (taking out the garbage, waxing the floors, mowing the lawn etc.)

14. He starts keeping an overnight bag in the car or at work. (If he tells you it's for the gym, look inside to see if it really contains workout clothes.)

15. He takes you to a "new" place but it's obvious from the way employees and patrons greet him that he's been there many times before.

16. He no longer wants to hold your hand when you're walking together. (He may actually pull his hand away from yours.)

17. His taste in music undergoes a radical change – from jazz to country and western, or from classical to reggae.

18. All before he was content to stay at home, now he wants a night out with the boys.

19. He does his own (or the family) laundry now. (To keep you from finding incriminating smells or stains on his clothing.)

20. He shows less interest in you and the children.

21. He embarks on a sudden self-improvement campaign – adult education classes, seminars, college courses or other intellectual pursuits.

22. He abandons his religious faith. (Since most religions condemn extra-marital affairs.)

23. He sneaks around acting secretive or suspicious.

24. He makes new male friends. (Since you already know his old friends, his cover could be blown if he claims to be hanging out with them.)

25. His evening or weekend classes last longer than they used to.

26. He stays up later than usual so he can sneak out, make phone calls in private, or send e-mail to his lover.

27. He acts restless when he's at home.

28. He's very short-tempered and impatient with the children (or your pets).

29. He starts acting like a single man again – hanging out late on evenings and weekends, running with a single crowd, neglecting his family obligations.

30. He now closes the bathroom door for privacy, when he used to leave it cracked or open all the way.

31. He pursues (or pretends to pursue) interests and activities that require him to be out of the house on evenings and weekends.

32. He moves away when you come near. He no longer wants you to touch or be physically close to him.

33. He goes to bed before you at night – either to avoid you or to call her from the bedroom.

34. He takes the dog on much longer walks than normal.

35. He makes excuses for not going out with you. He doesn't want to risk being seen with you by someone who has previously seen him with her.)

36. His daily habits have changed. He breaks his established routine for no apparent reason.

37. He gets a post office box for his personal use. (Check his key ring for a key on that says "USPS Do not Duplicate".)

38. He suddenly becomes involved in community or cultural affairs, sports activities, or new hobbies.

39. He exhibits a newfound interest in women's clothing—looking in catalogs and store windows that he'd normally ignore. (He's planning to buy his lover a gift.)

40. He used to avoid exercise, but now he's a regular at the gym. (Keep track of the days and times he claims to be working out.)

41. He starts doing things for you and the children that he wouldn't ordinarily do. (He's motivated by guilt.)

42. His sleep patterns change. He goes to bed earlier or later, or he gets up earlier each morning.

43. He loses his desire to do major home improvement projects (painting, renovation, landscaping, etc.).

44. He has no recollection of the errands he hurriedly left home to do.

45. He stops walking around the house nude or semi-nude to conceal incriminating marks on his body.

46. He starts taking you to new restaurants, museums, nightspots, etc. but seems to know an awful lot about them in advance.

47. He makes excuses to leave seasonal family gatherings (Thanksgiving, Christmas, New Year's, etc.) so he can drop by or call his lover to extend holiday greetings to her.

48. You go to a "new" bar, club, restaurant or nightspot and he's asked if he wants "his usual." (Obviously this isn't his first time there.)

49. He visits his friends more frequently, and spends more time with them than he does with you.

50. He no longer leaves his clothes lying around. Now he puts them away (to keep you from noticing suspicious odors or stains).

51. He frequently "forgets" to call at the time he said he'd call to check in.

52. He comes to bed long after he thinks you're asleep.

53. He starts frequenting places you never heard of before, and refuses to take you along.

54. His guilt prompts him to be more attentive to you and the children. (This usually happens in the early stages of an affair. Later his behavior will be just the opposite.)

55. He suddenly becomes involved in jogging, hiking, biking, weight lifting or other fitness related activities.

56. He wants an extra night out with the guys each week.

57. He comes home with a nasty attitude after a "night out with the guys."

58. He stops using his pet names for you or addressing you with terms of endearment.

59. He shows resentment or complains about having to attend family events.

60. He now flirts openly with women when he never did so before.

61. He overreacts when infidelity is depicted in the movies, on TV or in the news.

62. He's doing a lot of things that don't make sense or just don't seem to add up.

63. He stops wearing his wedding ring – that age-old sign of a cheating spouse.

64. He doesn't want to spend time alone with you. He insists on having other people around.

65. His friends start acting strangely (uneasy, uncomfortable or nervous) around you.

66. He neglects his hobbies or favorite pastimes.

67. He daydreams a lot. He's physically there but his mind is someplace else.

68. He starts watching X-rated videos.

69. He seems to be leading a separate life.

70. He starts reading books, when you've never seen him read anything other than a newspaper in the past.

71. His taste in reading changes. He starts reading a different genre (science fiction, mystery, self-help, historical fiction, etc.).

72. He spruces himself up to go to the gym or to hang out with the guys.

73. He rents a post office box but refuses to give you the extra key.

74. You no longer attend social events together because he insists on going alone.

75. He concocts all kinds of excuses to avoid attending preplanned social or family events.

76. He's taken up a time-consuming new hobby – one that doesn't interest you and requires him to be away from home.

77. You find coded entries in his date book or his Palm Pilot.

78. He claims to have lost or misplaced his wedding band.

79. He always "forgets" to wear his wedding band when he's out with the guys.

80. Those "urgent" errands he left home to take care of are still undone when he returns home hours later.

81. He always has excuses for why he couldn't complete the errands he left home to attend.

82. His taste in music undergoes a radical change.

83. He now gets enthusiastically involved in activities he once hated.

84. He'd rather read, watch TV or surf the Net than spend time interacting with you.

85. He carries grooming articles with him (toothbrush, deodorant, soap, cologne, hair brush or comb) when he goes out for the night.

86. He stops carrying pictures of you and the children in his wallet.

87. He comes home very late and sleeps someplace else (guest room, couch, family room) other than in bed with you.

88. He walks around in a daze.

89. He starts having his personal mail sent to the office.

90. He starts deliberately doing things to sabotage your relationship.

91. Lately he's been drinking or smoking a lot.

92. He removes his wedding band when he's getting a tan, to avoid having telltale tan lines on his finger when he takes off his ring to cheat.

Chapter 12

FINANCIAL AFFAIRS

Affairs cost money. If your husband has a lover, he'll want to wine her, dine her, entertain her and buy her occasional gifts. Sooner or later this will be reflected in the family finances. Stay alert for financial telltale signs.

1. Your monthly credit card statement shows charges for gifts (flowers, jewelry, lingerie, etc.) that you've never personally received (particularly during the holiday season.)

2. Your bank statement reveals that he's been making withdrawals without your knowledge.

3. He opens a new checking account in his name only.

4. He stops giving you money for household expenses.

5. You find out the bills haven't been paid.

6. You find out he's been paying rent on another apartment or making mortgage payments on another house.

7. The names of unfamiliar restaurants or nightspots appear on your credit card statement.

8. You find statements or receipts for a credit card you didn't even know he had.

9. His paycheck doesn't reflect the overtime he claims to be working.

10. There's an increase in his ATM withdrawals.

11. You find evidence (receipts, cancelled checks, money orders) that he has been paying someone else's bills.

12. He hides or "misplaces" bank statements or credit card bills to cover up his spending.

13. You find deposit slips or bank statements for a secret bank account in his name.

14. Lately he's been spending more than the usual amount of money on himself (clothing, cologne, toiletries, designer hair cuts, manicures, his car, etc.).

15. Money now becomes a major issue between you, when it never was before.

16. You find cancelled checks or money orders made out to his mistress.

17. He cashes in stocks and bonds without explaining why.

18. There's a sudden decrease in his disposable income — now he's always short of cash or broke.

19. He cleans out your joint bank account.

20. He no longer allows you to use the joint credit cards.

21. He becomes vague, evasive or secretive about his income or other financial matters.

22. He demands that you cut back on household expenses with no valid explanation why. (Affairs can be costly—he may need more money to maintain his infidelity.

23. His (or your joint) income tax return(s) reveal unexplained travel-related deductions.

24. He liquidates assets (real estate, coin or stamp collections, artwork, etc.) to provide additional spending money for his affair.

25. He keeps the family financial records on computer but won't give you the access code.

26. The transaction slips for his ATM withdrawals reveal that they were made at a suspicious time or location or on a suspicious date.

27. He starts charging up or "maxing out" all your joint credit cards.

28. You find out he's paying child support for his "love-child".

29. You discover that he's being blackmailed by a former lover or by someone who knows about his affair.

30. You notice that he's been spending more money than usual.

31. He stops questioning you about your purchases or spending habits (so you won't question him about his).

32. He suggests opening separate checking accounts.

33. You notice the gradual (or sudden) depletion of money from your joint checking or savings accounts.

34. He lies about his salary.

35. He cuts back on or eliminates luxury spending.

36. He transfers property to his parents, your in-laws or your children's names without a valid explanation.

37. He starts shifting savings or other investments around.

38. He starts transferring ownership of family assets without a valid reason.

39. You find deposit slips in his possession for someone else's bank account.

40. You find out that he and his lover have a joint bank account.

41. Your credit card statement shows numerous purchases made from women's boutiques, shoe stores or catalogs that you didn't make.

42. His lover attempts to extort money from you in return for leaving your husband alone.

43. He asks, suggests or insists that you assume financial responsibility for more or all of the household bills.

44. He suggests you get a job or ask for a promotion or raise to take some of the financial burden off himself.

45. He now deposits less money from his paycheck in the bank.

46. The two of you are on a tight budget, but new clothing keeps magically appearing in his wardrobe.

47. He claims business is in a slump, yet others in the same industry are prospering.

48. He cuts back on necessities for no apparent reason.

49. He's living an extravagant lifestyle while being stingy or frugal at home.

50. He puts in long hours on the job but you're still struggling to make ends meet at home.

51. He starts pawning items at the local pawn shop.

52. He hides his checkbook from you.

Chapter 13

TRAVEL

Your husband may not always be traveling for legitimate reasons. Even if he is, he may decide to combine business with a little pleasure. Travel affords him a unique opportunity to cheat away from prying eyes.

1. He no longer takes or invites you along on business trips.

2. He's evasive or vague about the details of his business trip.

3. Lately his business trips have been lasting longer than before. (He may be padding his business trips by adding an extra day before or after so he can spend that time with his lover.

4. He attends a "business conference" that nobody else at his company knows anything about.

5. He now wants the two of you to take separate vacations.

6. He's unreachable by phone when he's out of town.

7. He told you he was going on a fishing/rafting/camping/hunting trip with the guys, but you find out he's the only one who left town.

8. You call his hotel room and a woman answers.

9. He takes more than his usual number of business trips or makes frequent unscheduled trips out of town.

10. He refuses to let you to drop him off or pick him up at the airport for his trip. (His lover may be meeting him there.)

11. There's a nervousness or heightened anxiety about him when he tells you about an upcoming "business" trip.

12. He says he's taking a business trip, but all he packs are casual clothes. (shorts, jeans, T-shirts, swimming trunks).

13. He gives you a cell phone number instead of a hotel number to reach him when he's out of town. (He could be trying to conceal his location.)

14. He's not registered at any of the hotels in the city where he said he'd be. (He may be staying with his lover at an apartment or a private home.)

15. He encourages you to take trips without him or keeps suggesting that you visit a distant relative, attend a business conference or take a vacation with your girlfriends. (He wants you out of the way so he can spend time with his lover.)

16. He repeatedly talks about going on a camping, rafting, fishing or hunting trip with the guys. (He may be setting up an alibi.)

17. Lately he "forgets" to tell you where and how to reach him when he's out of town.

18. He stays at a different hotel than the one he told you.

19. The trip he says he took for business reasons turns out to have been a vacation with his lover.

20. He returns home empty-handed from what he said was a fishing trip with the guys, and his fishing gear looks untouched.

21. Your Caller ID registers a local number when he calls home, indicating that he never really left town.

22. Your Caller ID indicates that he's in a different city, state or country than where he said he would be.

23. He doesn't answer his cell phone in the evenings when he's out of town. He's only reachable during the day.

24. He said he was going on a fishing or camping trip with the guys, but he neglected to take his gear.

25. When he's traveling, he insists on calling you, rather than having you phone him. (He doesn't want you keeping tabs on him or knowing where he is.)

26. He calls to tell you he has to stay an extra day or two on his business trip, but is changing hotels because they're overbooked.

27. His (or your joint) tax return(s) reveal unexplained deductions for travel expenses.

Chapter 14

PERSONALITY OR BEHAVIORAL CHANGES

Be alert for changes in your husband's attitude, personality or behavior. Whether drastic or subtle, changes of this type are often an indication of infidelity.

1. He becomes quiet and introspective, moody or withdrawn.

2. He's happier, friendlier or more cheerful.

3. He's now evasive or secretive about his activities.

4. He's a lot easier to get along with now.

5. He becomes weepy, teary-eyed, or overly sentimental for no apparent reason. (His guilt is eating away at him.)

6. He becomes more talkative.

7. He becomes belligerent or argumentative, constantly picking fights with you.

8. He acts more confident, more self-assured.

9. He's impatient with you and the kids.

10. He acts like he's annoyed just to be in your presence.

11. He becomes touchy or defensive.

12. He seems overwrought or unduly stressed for no apparent reason.

13. He becomes extremely critical even of trivial things.

14. He tries to act younger.

15. He becomes cranky, short-tempered and generally disagreeable.

16. He becomes very possessive about his wallet, appointment book, pocket calendar, briefcase, Palm Pilot, cell phone, pager, backpack or other personal possessions. (He's trying to hide something.)

17. He seems to be "walking on air."

18. His whole disposition changes if you ask him to stay home or take you along with him when he's going out.

19. He seems emotionally aloof.

20. He changes almost overnight from an introvert into an extrovert, or vice versa.

21. He resumes dating behavior. (Remember how he used to act when the two of you were dating?)

22. He becomes secretive about seemingly minor aspects of his life.

23. He overreacts to innocent questions.

24. His personality has changed. Lately he just hasn't been himself.

25. He's always in a foul mood.

26. He's extremely irritable. Everything seems to get on his nerves.

27. He becomes sullen or morose.

28. He's indifferent to the things going on around him.

29. He has an air of indifference about him.

30. He becomes very forgetful.

31. He develops a cold, uncaring attitude.

32. He becomes very selfish.

33. He's more easily offended.

34. He seems nervous, tense, on-edge.

35. His energy level increases.

36. He exhibits extreme anxiety.

Chapter 15

ABSENCES

Affairs generally require a man to invest a considerable amount of time. Your husband's absences will become more frequent as he tries to steal time to spend with his lover.

---

1. His absences occur at specific times, intervals, or on specific days of the week. Log them into a journal to see if you can detect a pattern.

2. Now he feels compelled to explain to you where he's going or where he's been, even though he never used to account for his time before.

3. He gets defensive if you ask him where he's going or where he's been.

4. He has all kinds of new obligations that require him to be away from home.

5. He disappears for hours at a time with no plausible explanation for where he's been.

6. He sneaks out of the house while you're busy with the kids so you can't ask him where he's going.

7. He gives you such a detailed explanation for where he's going and why, you know he couldn't possibly be telling you the truth.

8. If you insist on going with him when he goes out, he changes his mind and stays home.

9. He leaves the house without telling you where he's going.

10. He becomes vague, touchy, evasive, nervous or defensive if you ask him anything about his schedule for the week.

11. There are inconsistencies in his explanations for why he's always gone.

12. He says he's been going to the gym to work out, but you have yet to see any visible change in his weight, muscle tone or his physique.

13. He claims he's going to visit a relative or friend, but when you check you find out he's not there.

14. He concocts all kinds of excuses or reasons to justify why he has to go out alone.

15. His alibi sounds *too* perfect.

16. He ignores you or pretends not to hear you when you ask him where he's going.

17. He pretends he's taking the kids with him, but drops them at the sitter's (or with a relative or friend), then goes off on his own.

18. He comes back from watching a ball game with the guys, but can't tell you anything about the highlights of the game when you ask.

19. When he leaves home to run a simple errand, he's gone much longer than he should be.

20. His excuses and explanations for his absences become increasingly more creative or outrageous.

21. He acts annoyed, rude, nasty, or hostile when you ask if you can go with him.

22. He's been spending more time than usual away from home—always with plausible-sounding explanations (a business trip, overtime at work, trips to the corner store, walking the dog, running errands, hanging out with his friends).

23. He "runs errands" at odd, unusual or inappropriate times.

24. He makes flimsy, obviously phony excuses if you ask where he's going or where he's been.

25. He makes excessive use of "doctor's or dentist's appointments" to account for his time away from home.

26. He goes to the gym much earlier or stays much later. (Check to see if he's really working out, and if so, with whom?)

27. He disappears for days at a time.

28. He stays out all night.

29. He tells you he's going shopping, but returns home with no merchandise. There's a limit to how many times a man can go window-shopping, especially if he hates to shop.

30. Lately he's been doing an excessive amount of "errand running" or "walking the dog."

31. When you ask him where he's going, he refuses to tell you.

32. He leaves abruptly for appointments or meetings that he "forgot" to tell you about.

33. He said he was going to the store to get a specific item but he returned home empty-handed, and can't even remember what he left home to get.

34. He's not around at the usual times; he seems to be out more than normal.

35. He sneaks in after you're asleep so you won't know how long he's been gone.

36. He takes an unusually long time to drive the baby sitter home.

37. He disappears during social gatherings.

38. He frequently uses running into an old classmate or army buddy as his excuse for coming home late.

39. He uses evening or weekend classes to account for his time away from home. Did he actually register for a class? Is he still attending or did he register and drop out?

Chapter 16

TELEPHONE TIP-OFFS

Illicit affairs depend on repeated contact; many of which take place by phone. These telltale signs are relatively easy to find. Many men take the risk of calling their lovers from home or having their lovers call them on their home phone. Many wives (like me) discover their husband's infidelity either directly or indirectly via the telephone.

1. He leaves your presence so he can make (or take) phone calls in private, now carrying on most of his phone conversations behind closed doors.

2. If you're around when he answers the phone he acts awkward, nervous or ill-at-ease.

3. He dashes for the phone every time it rings.

4. When you ask him who just called, he lies. (Dial *69 or check the Caller ID.)

5. He uses his cell phone around the house.

6. You catch him whispering or mumbling into the phone.

7. The same unfamiliar number shows up repeatedly on your phone bill or Caller-ID. (If you don't have Caller ID, *get it!* Hook it up to a phone jack behind the couch, underneath a table or otherwise out of sight.)

8. He quickly terminates phone conversations when you come in. Whenever you enter a room and find him on the phone, he always seems to be just hanging up.

9. He positions the cordless phone so he's the only one who can reach it when it rings.

10. Before he makes a phone call, he checks to see where you are.

11. He starts using phone cards to avoid having certain numbers show up on his home or cell phone bill.

12. There is a sudden increase in "wrong numbers." (Dial *69 or get Caller ID service to see where these calls are coming from.)

13. He used to routinely check in with you by phone. Now he doesn't call at all.

14. You receive an unprecedented number of suspicious phone calls – wrong numbers, hang-ups, no one on the other end, unfamiliar female voices, blocked numbers, etc.

15. He has cryptic conversations when he talks on the phone. He answers in monosyllables or appears to be speaking in code.

16. You overhear an incriminating conversation between him and his lover when you pick up the extension to make a call.

17. A female answers when you press "redial" or dial *69.

18. He tries to avoid answering the phone at certain times. (He's afraid it might be his lover.)

19. Hoping to break up your marriage, his lover calls and tells you about the affair. (Don't fall for her little tricks.)

20. He keeps "forgetting" to give you a phone number so you can reach him when he's out of town.

21. He makes frequent or lengthy phone calls to a female friend, co-worker or business associate.

22. He hides or "misplaces" the phone bill to keep you from knowing what numbers he calls. (You can request a print-out from the phone company of all the calls—local and long distance—made from your number during a given period of time.)

23. He buys a cell phone for his personal use.

24. He glances around suspiciously to see where you are while he's talking on the phone.

25. He only checks his voice mail or his answering machine when you're not around to overhear. If you know his code (or can get it) check his messages when he's not in.

26. When he's out, he calls you more frequently than before. (He's checking to see where you are so he won't run into you while he's with her.)

27. He makes or receives phone calls at odd or unexpected times (very late at night or early in the morning).

28. He carries on a lengthy conversation with a "wrong number."

29. His lover's husband or boyfriend calls and tells you what's been going on behind your back.

30. He immediately picks up the phone to call his lover as soon as you leave home (or whenever you take a shower or bath). Double back and you'll catch him in the act.

31. He keeps casting anxious glances at the phone or the Caller ID.

32. He behaves suspiciously after the phone rings a single ring. (He concocts an excuse to run an errand shortly afterwards or he disappears to make a private call.)

33. He calls you at work to find out what time you're coming home – so he and his lover can make plans for after work.

34. On nights when he works late, he's unreachable by phone.

35. You call his hotel room when he's out of town and a woman answers the phone.

36. He no longer leaves a number where you can reach him when he's not at home or at work.

37. You find a cell phone you didn't even know he had.

38. He has the phone bill mailed to him at work to keep you from seeing the numbers he calls.

39. There's a significant increase in his phone calls *to* or *from* a particular person.

40. He now takes hours instead of minutes to return your calls.

41. He always calls a certain close female friend to share the special events in his life.

42. If you ask him who just called, he gets nervous, evasive or vague.

43. When he calls home, the Caller ID indicates that he's lying to you about where he is.

44. He makes late-night phone calls when he thinks you're asleep.

45. He starts making frequent use of pay phones.

46. When he's out, he always calls from a blocked number when checking in so you can't trace the call.

47. He calls to verify that you're still where you said you'd be so he won't get caught by surprise.

48. You receive an anonymous phone call telling you he's cheating.

49. He has lengthy phone conversations with a female you don't know.

50. You hear suspicious or inappropriate sounds in the background when he calls home to check in.

51. His lover calls and asks you to give him a divorce so he can marry her. (It's common for a man to tell his mistress he can't marry her because his wife won't give him a divorce.)

52. You overhear him on the phone setting up an alibi with one of his friends.

53. There are messages on his answering machine or his voice mail from unidentified females. Use his code to play back his messages when he's not home.

54. You get repeated calls and hang-ups in a short span of time that stop only after he answers the phone. (Usually an indication of an unstable or immature lover.)

55. Your phone bill shows repeated calls to an unfamiliar number. (A word of caution: If you're going to check out unfamiliar phone numbers use a pay phone, a calling card, or dial *67 to block your number. The other person may have Caller ID.)

56. You call a phone number you suspect belongs to his lover, and he happens to answer the phone.

57. You overhear him on the phone sharing personal information or intimate details of his life with a so-called female "friend."

58. He now makes it his business to answer the phone before you do.

59. He gives you a fictitious phone number to contact him while he's out. (Always check the number.)

60. Suspicious phone calls (hang-ups, wrong numbers, blocked calls, no one on the other end, etc.) only occur at certain times or the day or night – or only on certain days of the week. Write down the days and   times to see if you can detect a pattern.

61. He no longer returns your calls – he says he was too busy or he forgot.

62. Your Caller ID shows an unusually large number of blocked calls.

63. You start receiving phone calls from a scorned or rejected lover of his.

64. He won't give you the number to his private line at work.

65. He adds another phone line at home (ostensibly for "business use") in his study or another place in the home where he he is the only one with has access to it.

66. He now checks in frequently when he's out, to keep you from trying to reach him and finding out he's not where he said he would be.

67. When he thinks you're too busy to notice, he tries to sneak in a call to his lover.

68. You call his hotel when he's out of town and you're told he's not registered there.

69. Shortly before or after he leaves the house, someone always calls and hangs up. (It may be his lover checking to see if he's still coming or to confirm that he's already on his way.)

70. When he calls to says he'll be late, he's whispering into the phone or talking in an unusually low tone. (His lover is probably nearby and he doesn't want to be overheard.)

71. When you say "I love you" to him over the phone, he now refuses to respond in kind. (His lover is with him and he can't speak freely.)

72. All of a sudden he wants to change your home phone number to a new or unlisted number.

73. He erases messages from the answering machine before you get a chance to play them back.

74. He no longer returns your calls promptly when you call him on his pager.

75. When you return from an errand and press redial on your phone, a woman's voice answers.

76. He calls a female "friend" several times a day.

Chapter 17

CAR CLUES

Your husband's car (or the family car) can be a rich source of telltale signs. The glove compartment, car seats (underneath and between), the tire well, the underside of the visor, the ashtray, the side pockets or compartments, under the floor mats and other nooks and crannies can reveal a wealth of information. Keep your eyes open and stay alert.

---

1. The passenger seat has been has been moved from its normal position or readjusted for someone other than you.

2. You find a change of clothing hidden in the trunk.

3. The air conditioning vents on the passenger side have been repositioned at the wrong angle for you.

4. You find hairs of a different color, length, or texture from yours on the headrest of the passenger seat.

5. The car radio is tuned to a different station from the one he usually listens to.

6. You find lingerie (panties, a bra, pantihose) in the glove compartment.

7. You find packages of condoms in the car. (Look in the glove compartment or underneath the seat.)

8. You discover empty condom wrappers or used condoms in the car.

9. You find suspicious-looking white stains on the car seats.

10. You see his car parked in some incriminating place – a restaurant, a strange neighborhood, in a lover's lane or the parking lot of a motel.

11. You find a bottle of his favorite cologne hidden in the glove compartment, the trunk or under the seat in the car.

12. The vanity mirror on the passenger side has been left down. (His lover may have needed to check her hair or refresh her make-up before leaving the car.)

13. There are cigarette butts in the car ashtray and he doesn't smoke. (If they have lipstick on them it's a dead giveaway.)

14. The odometer shows that he used the car while you were asleep last night. Check the mileage before going to bed. (Write it down so you won't forget). Recheck it in the morning before he leaves for work.

15. He starts keeping breath mints, gum or ChapStick in the car to ensure that his mouth is always in "kissable" condition.

16. You find CD's or cassettes in the car for a type of music neither of you normally listen to.

17. You find a box of cleaning wipes concealed in the car (for cleaning up after sex).

18. His car, which usually looks like a junk pile on wheels, is now being kept immaculately clean.

19. He starts keeping a blanket in the trunk.

20. You find toiletries and grooming aids (deodorant, toothbrush, toothpaste, mouthwash soap, a shaver/razor, etc.) hidden in the car.

21. He frequently uses car trouble (flat tires, out of gas, transmission problems) as an excuse for coming home late.

22. He suddenly starts using car deodorizers.

23. He keeps a travel-size bottle of Febreze (or a similar fabric odor neutralizer) in the car to get rid of incriminating smells on the car seats or his clothing.

24. The credit card receipt for his gas shows that it was purchased from a location where he had no valid reason to be.

25. The odometer shows too many extra miles. Make note of the number of miles from home to work. Write down the mileage with the dates. Does the mileage coincide with his alleged daily destination? Careful records will help you determine whether his lover lives nearby or a considerable distance away.

26. Someone reports that his car was seen parked in a location where it shouldn't have been at the time.

27. He gets involved in a sudden flurry of activity, washing and waxing his car.

28. His odometer shows *less* mileage than it should. (He says he's going across town, but from the mileage shown, he couldn't have gone much farther than around the block.)

29. The parking ticket he got indicates he was in a location where he had no legitimate reason to be. (Check the date and time.)

30. He takes his car to the car wash more frequently than before.

31. He buys or decides to buy a flashier car.

32. The ashtray in his car contains a different brand of cigarette from the one he smokes.

33. You find a cell phone or pager hidden in the car that you didn't even know he had.

34. You find a gift for his lover hidden in the car.

35. You find an article of women's clothing in the car that's not yours.

36. The paper towels or facial tissues you keep in the car are disappearing at a rapid rate.

37. He suddenly buys new or replacement seat covers for the car. (Did the old ones have incriminating stains?)

38. You find unfamiliar jewelry (earrings, watch, necklace) in the car.

39. He removes his car keys from your key ring.

40. There are cigarette burns in the car upholstery and neither of you smoke.

Chapter 18

SEX

Be alert for any changes in the frequency or the quality of your sex life together. Most important of all: if you suspect your husband of having an affair, take steps to protect yourself. Do not put yourself at risk for HIV/AIDS, herpes or other sexually transmitted diseases.

1. Though you can't quite put your finger on it, sex between you somehow seems different.

2. He doesn't initiate sex anymore. (The two of you only make love when you approach him.)

3. He avoids having sex with you by coming to bed only after he thinks you've fallen asleep.

4. You discover a hidden stash of condoms. (Don't let him know you found them. Count them and write down the dates they disappear. Cross check it with his absences.)

5. He no longer makes eye contact with you when you have sex.

6. He changes his lovemaking technique. (His lover taught him a new trick.)

7. Your sex life declines–either gradually tapering off or coming to a screeching halt. (Cheating husbands will sometimes avoid having sex with their wives out of a misplaced sense of loyalty to their lovers.)

8. The condoms you normally use for birth control are disappearing at a rate faster than is warranted by the frequency of your sex together. (Count them and periodically check how many there are on a given date. . Write down the dates and numbers so you won't get confused.)

9. He no longer kisses you when he makes love to you.

10. Your sex life increases. He wants sex more often. He displays a renewed interest in sex. Some men become so aroused by their extramarital affairs that the excitement carries over into their marriage.

11. He buys and studies sex manuals and related materials.

12. He starts wearing condoms despite the fact that you normally use another method of birth control or no birth control at all.

13. Your sex life gets a new surge of energy–new techniques, new places, new positions or new variations of some kind. (Either he's learning from her, or he's practicing his techniques on you in preparation for her.)

14. He switches to a different brand or type of condoms.

15. He comes up with all kinds of excuses for not having sex with you–too tired, too stressed, headache, backache, etc. (Either he's too worn out from his lover; or he's too ashamed or too guilt-ridden to make love to you.)

16. He now skips foreplay or afterplay and you sense that he's only having sex out of a sense of obligation to you.

17. He inadvertently calls you by her name while he's making love to you.

18. You find a hidden stash of sexually oriented items in his car, luggage, the back of his closet or drawer (spermicidal suppositories, AstroGlide, KY Jelly, vibrators, dildoes, pornography, etc.).

19. He picks fights at bedtime so he can avoid having sex with you by sleeping on the couch or in the guest room.

20. You find a condom in his pocket, wallet, briefcase or luggage.

21. His lover tells you she's been sexually intimate with him.

22. He finally stops bugging you for more frequent sex or for whatever sexual variation he's always craved. If he suddenly stops asking, check things out—maybe someone else is fulfilling his request.

23. He turns down sex when you try to initiate it.

24. There's less excitement, less passion in your lovemaking.

25. You find empty condom wrappers (or used condoms) in your home, the car, the garage, his office etc.

26. Sex between you has become very mechanical. He performs like his heart's not really in it.

27. He insists that you start using birth control–the pill, a diaphragm or an IUD.

28. He makes excuses, or flat-out refuses to come to bed when you do.

29. You find out he has an illegitimate child.

30. He starts taking Viagra.

31. You find lipstick or make-up stains on his underwear or his private parts.

32. He starts watching X-rated videos.

33. You find dried semen stains on his clothing or his car seats.

34. He can no longer achieve or maintain an erection.

35. He starts asking for unusual "bedroom favors".

36. You walk in on him having sex with someone else. (Come home unexpectedly one day.) If you find this telltale sign, it's the only sign you need.

37. Worst of all—and usually a definite sign of cheating—you contract a sexually transmitted disease.

Chapter 19

EATING HABITS

This is an area that women usually overlook when checking for telltale signs. Your husband's eating habits can be influenced or affected by his lover. Without even realizing it, he may develop a preference for the type of food she eats, the way she likes her food prepared or the type of restaurants in which she likes to eat. These are the kinds of telltale signs it would rarely occur to him to conceal.

---

1. His table manners suddenly improve.

2. At restaurants he orders food or drinks you've never known him to order before.

3. He starts complaining about your cooking.

4. He develops a taste for certain delicacies or various gourmet foods. (Find out who introduced him to these things.)

5. Overnight he becomes knowledgeable about various vintages of wine.

6. He goes on a health food kick.

7. He's never hungry when he comes home; lately he's always too full to eat. (He's been taking his lover out to dinner or eating at her place.)

8. He stops putting ketchup or hot sauce all over everything he eats.

9. He takes you to a more upscale class of restaurant than he did in the past.

10. He starts checking food labels to find out the nutritional content of what he eats.

11. He develops a sudden fondness for a specific ethnic food (Thai, Greek, French, Brazilian, Mexican, etc.)Where has he eaten this food before?

12. He announces that he's becoming a vegetarian.

13. He starts telling you how to season his food.

14. He comes home ravenously hungry from what was supposed to have been a business dinner or banquet.

15. He brings home something unusual (a different cut of meat, a new type of vegetable) for you to cook.

16. He criticizes *your* table manners.

17. He starts asking why you never cook a particular type of food or use a specific method of food preparation.

18. He stops drinking coffee and switches to drinking herbal tea.

19. Now when you dine out, he interrogates the waiter about the ingredients or how the food is prepared.

20. Out of the blue he asks you to cook him a dish that you've never prepared for him before.

21. He suddenly decides to fast or go on a strict diet.

22. He rearranges the silverware or tells you the table is improperly set.

23. All of a sudden he develops a liking for a type of food he previously refused to eat.

24. He now goes to work early on certain days so he can have breakfast in the morning—with his lover.

25. He graduates from drinking regular coffee to drinking cappuccino, latte, espresso or gourmet/premium blends.

26. Suddenly he only wants to eat salads.

27. He comes home with new recipes he wants you to try.

28. He stops asking you to cook his favorite foods.

29. He rarely eats meals at home anymore.

30. Instead of his usual hearty appetite, he merely picks at his food.

31. He has a sudden abundance of dinner meetings.

Chapter 20

SMELLS AND TASTES

Every person has his or her own unique smell or taste. You may be oblivious to it until it becomes replaced with something else. Pay close attention if your husband smells or tastes "different," or if something in your home or car just doesn't smell "right." It may warrant closer investigation.

---

1. He comes home with the smell of an unfamiliar perfume.

2. He comes home smelling like the perfume you normally wear, but he couldn't possibly have picked it up from you. (Some men buy their lovers a bottle of their wife's favorite perfume so she won't be suspicious if she smells it on his clothing.)

3. You detect sexual smells on his body.

4. You detect the lingering smell of an unfamiliar perfume on your pillowcases.

5. Sexual odors may be detectable in his moustache or beard if he engages in oral sex with his lover.

6. His kisses taste like cigarettes but he doesn't smoke.

7. He comes home smelling freshly showered at the end of a long day at work or after a "night out with the guys".

8. He smells of a different brand of soap or deodorant than the one you use at home.

9. He comes home smelling faintly of another woman's body.

10. You catch him spraying his clothing with a fabric odor neutralizer like Febreze to rid his clothing of incriminating odors.

11. The car reeks of sex.

12. He puts on cologne to run errands, "work out at the gym" or "hang out with the guys."

13. Your non-smoking husband comes home with cigarette smoke in his hair or on his clothing.

14. He makes a point of wearing cologne only on certain days of the week, or on the days when he has to work late.

15. You come home from work and find your bedroom smelling like sex.

16. You detect an uncharacteristic body odor or unfamiliar smell on his clothing or his person.

17. He keeps a travel-size bottle of Febreze (or other odor-neutralizing product) in his briefcase, back pack, car or his desk at work.

18. His genital area smells like chocolate, strawberries, wine or some other food.

19. He has the smell of alcohol on his breath even though he doesn't drink.

20. He comes home with a pungent smell on his fingers, hands or genitals.

21. He comes in smelling subtly (or reeking) of alcohol.

Chapter 21

INVASION OF YOUR HOME

It's not uncommon for a man who's cheating to invite his lover to his home. When this happens, it's not unheard of for a lover to leave personal items behind— sometimes intentionally, for his wife to find. You will usually find evidence in your bedroom or bathroom if another woman has been in your home while you were away. You should also check other areas of your home for telltale signs.

---

1. You find semen stains on your bed but you haven't had sex with him. (Turn the bed back and check.)

2. You find unfamiliar personal articles in your home–a compact, lipstick a different shade from yours, earrings, hair combs, etc.

3. You discover used towels or soiled sheets in the laundry basket or clothes hamper. (A dead giveaway if they contain make-up or semen stains.)

4. You find freshly laundered towels or sheets in the linen closet or in the dryer. (He may have tried to cover his tracks.)

5. The guest room appears to have been used.

6. For the first time since you've been married he voluntarily puts fresh linen on the bed.

7. There's the lingering smell of a strange perfume on your pillowcases.

8. You find panties, a bra or pantihose under the mattress, or underneath the bed or between the cushions on the couch. (Common places the other woman will deliberately plant "souvenirs" for an unsuspecting wife to find.)

9. There are make-up stains on your pillowcases. (First, make sure they're not yours.)

10. He puts fresh towels in the bathroom when he's never done so before.

11. Unfamiliar toiletries (soap, shampoo, hair conditioner, toothpaste, deodorant) or make-up turn up in your bathroom.

12. Items of entertainment (CDs, cassettes, videotapes, DVDs or even books) may be misplaced, rearranged, out of their usual order or missing.

13. You find unfamiliar articles of women's clothing in your home. (Make sure they're not yours or your daughter's.)

14. Kitchen articles (dishes, silverware, glasses, cooking utensils) may be misplaced or rearranged.

15. Some of your clothing or accessories are missing.

16. You find unfamiliar CDs, cassettes, videos or DVD's mixed in with yours.

17. Bed linen or towels have been replaced on the wrong shelf.

18. You find lipstick-stained cigarette butts in your home and you're a non-smoker.

19. You find an article of clothing in your home that is not your style or size.

20. You find a bottle of Febreze hidden in the bedroom or the guest room.

21. You find evidence that he's entertained someone in your absence – a pair of wine glasses in the sink or dishwasher, an empty wine bottle, the remnants of a meal for two in the garbage, etc.

22. You find an X-rated video left in your VCR.

Chapter 22

GIFTS

Be especially vigilant around the times of the year when gifts are usually exchanged. During the holidays and various other times throughout the year, you may find gifts or cards hidden around your home or in the car. Receipts for gifts may turn up shortly before or after Christmas or Valentine's Day.

1. You find bills or receipts among his personal possessions for gifts that were obviously given to someone else, since he didn't give them to you.

2. You find a gift that's obviously intended for someone other than you. (A size obviously too small or too large for you, or a color or style he knows you'd never wear.)

3. He tries to pass off gifts from his lover (clothing, electronics, and personal items) as things that he purchased for himself. Ask him to show you the receipts.

4. Out of the blue, he buys you a major gift (car, new house, outrageously expensive piece of jewelry or the equivalent) that he was dead-set against buying you before. (Usually done out of guilt.)

5. He's always buying little gifts for a particular female friend.

6. He now gives you a check, cash or a gift certificate, because he too busy with his lover to pick out a gift for you.

7. The gifts he's given you lately reflect a new level of taste or insight regarding women. Before he'd give you kitchen appliances or items for the house, now he gives you jewelry, lingerie or gifts of more personal nature.

8. He no longer forgets to buy you a gift for Valentine's Day, Christmas, etc. (Since he has to buy a gift for his lover, he automatically buys one for you too.)

9. He stops giving you gifts because he's spending all his disposable income on his lover.

10. He always buys anniversary or birthday gifts for you now. (His lover reminds him, or shops for him or with him so they can keep you appeased.)

11. A husband who was never much of a gift giver starts showering you with "guilt gifts."

12. He buys an inappropriately or outrageously expensive gift for a female coworker or casual friend.

13. He buys gifts for another woman's children.

14. He displays a newfound interest in women's clothing and jewelry, scrutinizing store windows or catalogs that he'd normally ignore. (He's looking for a gift for his lover.)

15. You find a thank you card or note to him from his lover for a gift he gave her.

16. His gift-giving style changes—he now gives you gifts of a higher quality.

17. Lately he's been receiving gifts from someone you don't know.

18. Despite the limitations of the family budget, new clothing keeps appearing in his wardrobe. (His lover is giving him gifts.)

19. He buys a bottle of your favorite perfume but doesn't give it to you. A man will often have his lover wear the same perfume as his wife to keep her from being suspicious.

Chapter 23

COMPUTER USE

It's common these days for a cheating husband to use e-mail to communicate with his lover. Some of the telltale signs below may also be an indication that he's involved in an online or cyber affair. Don't take this lightly. Cyber affairs can do just as much damage to your marriage as the real thing. Though they may not involve sexual contact, the emotional attachment can be extremely strong. Online affairs can easily progress from the computer screen to physical reality.

---

1. When he's at the computer he acts very secretive about what he's doing online.

2. He's constantly online with female "friends."

3. He insists on privacy while he surfs the Net.

4. He starts sharing intimate information about himself with an online female friend.

5. He habitually gets instant messages from the same female(s) when he's online.

6. He anxiously hovers around the computer when you're online. (He's afraid you'll get an instant message intended for him.)

7. He deletes histories and files to cover his online tracks.

8. He closes his laptop whenever you enter the room.

9. He sets up a separate e-mail account for himself on the family computer.

10. He keeps changing his passwords. (What is he trying to hide?)

11. He switches computer screens, closes or hides windows when you walk in.

12. He moves the computer to more private area of the house–the garage, his workshop, the attic, the basement, a closet-to conceal what he's doing online.

13. He heads for the computer as soon as he wakes up for a pre-work e-mail exchange with his lover.

14. He stays up late using the computer long after you've gone to bed.

15. He signs up for multiple e-mail accounts.

16. You attempt to access his e-mail and find that he changed the password without telling you. (Peek over his shoulder when he enters his password and check his e-mail when he's not around.)

17. You find incriminating e-mail(s) to him from another woman.

18. He becomes obsessed with online chat rooms and insists on chatting alone.

19. He now password-protects his computer to deny you access.

20. He adds alternate screen names to the Internet account.

21. He becomes sexually aroused as he chats online or surfs the Net.

22. He spends an excessive amount of time in sexually-oriented chat rooms or in private member rooms.

23. He keeps nervously glancing over his shoulder to see if you're watching what he's doing online.

24. He sends or receives e-mails which contain erotic undertones.

25. He goes through frantic mouse-clicking when you walk in.

26. He attempts to conceal his password from you when he logs on.

27. The computer has become more important to him than his relationship with you.

28. While you're online you intercept an incriminating instant message from a female that's clearly intended for him.

29. He's constantly e-mailing people who are unfamiliar to you.

30. He shuts down the computer when you enter the room.

Chapter 24

CELL PHONES
AND PAGERS /BEEPERS

Technological advances like cell phones and pagers make it easier for husbands to cheat on their wives. But it also makes it easier for them to get caught.

1. Shortly after receiving a call on his cell phone or a message on his pager, he remembers an important errand he has to run.

2. He leaves your presence to talk on his cell phone or return a call from his pager in privacy.

3. Lately he's become very possessive about his cell phone or pager–hiding it, locking it away, not allowing you to use it, always keeping it in his possession.

4. He becomes evasive or gets flustered if you ask him who just called or paged him.

5. He tries to conceal the numbers on his cell phone or the messages on his pager from your view. (Try to check the numbers before he erases them.)

6. You find unfamiliar numbers programmed into his cell phone or pager.

7. You see numerical codes on his beeper. (777, 411, 911, etc.) Or 568-3968, which translates to "love you" or 647-7968 "miss you."

8. He buys a pager or a cell phone for his personal use.

9. He glances at you nervously if you're near him when his pager goes off or his cell phone rings.

10. When he's in your presence, he turns off the sound on his cell phone or pager so you won't know when he gets a call.

11. He receives a cell phone call or a page from a female (coworker, neighbor, or acquaintance) who has no legitimate reason to know his personal number.

12. He always keeps his cell phone or pager on except for the times you're trying to reach him. Then somehow, it's mysteriously "off".

13. He turns off his cell phone or pager to keep you from reaching him and tells you the battery was low.

14. His cell phone bills increase every month.

15. His cell phone bill shows repeated calls to or from an unfamiliar number.

16. He has his cell phone bill mailed to his job so you can't track what numbers or how often he calls.

17. He won't allow you to use his cell phone or pager.

18. He turns off his cell phone when he comes home so his calls will be directed to his voice mail. This way he can retrieve them when you're not around.

19. You find out the cell phone or pager that he told you was supplied by his job was actually bought by him for his personal use.

20. He refuses to give you his cell phone number—everyone else seems to have it but you.

21. The only way you can reach him when he's out of town is through his cell phone or pager. (He doesn't want you to know where he is.)

22. He "accidentally" (or intentionally) leaves his cell phone in the car at night when he comes home, to avoid dealing with incriminating calls.

23. His cell phone never seems to work (accidentally turned off, forgot to turn it on, battery low) on the nights he has to work late.

24. You find a cell phone that you didn't even know he had.

25. His cell phone or pager rings in the wee hours of the morning.

26. He used to return your calls promptly when you paged him. Now hours pass before he calls you back.

27. He uses his cell phone around the house.

28. He forgets to turn off his cell phone or pager and receives an incriminating call.

PHYSICAL EVIDENCE

Sometimes there's physical evidence just waiting to be found. Check your husband's wallet, his pants or jacket pockets, his desk or dresser drawers, the wastepaper basket, his closet shelves, the floor in the back of his closet, the garage, his study, filing cabinets, his workshop, his toolbox or any place else you can think of. Keep your eyes open. You'll be surprised at what you can find.

1. You find another woman's picture in his wallet. (Look between or behind his business cards or other pictures.)

2. Evidence turns up (cancelled checks, receipts, a lease in his or someone else's name) to indicate he's maintaining a separate residence.

3. You find drugstore receipts for condoms. (Check the date, time and location they were purchased to see if they coincide with his absences.)

4. You find a receipt or credit card bill from a hotel, motel, or bed and breakfast inn.

5. You discover a new or unfamiliar key on his key ring. (It could be the key to her place or to their secret hideaway.)

6. You find ticket stubs from movies, concerts, plays, or other places he's taken her. Write down the dates for future reference.

7. You find evidence of sexual activity—empty condom wrappers or used condoms that he thought he'd disposed of.

8. There are dried semen stains on his clothing or his car seats.

9. You notice lipstick or make-up stains on his underwear (or on his private parts).

10. You find incriminating marks (scratches, love bites, black-and- blue marks hickeys, etc.) on his body that he can't explain.

11. There are dog or cat hairs on his clothing but you don't have a pet. (Check the back of his shirt or jacket, the seat and cuffs of his pants and the bottom of his socks.)

12. You find florist or jewelry receipts for gifts you didn't get.

13. You discover incriminating e-mail, notes, cards, or love letters.

14. You come across suspicious entries in his appointment book—first or last names only, initials, coded entries.

15. You find a birthday card or thank-you note to him from his lover.

16. You find airline tickets, stubs or receipts indicating that he took or plans to take a trip with someone else. Check the dates against your evidence journal.

17. You find women's jewelry, lingerie, clothing or other personal articles in your home or car that don't belong to you.

18. There are stray hairs of a different color, length, or texture from yours in his car, on his clothing or among his personal possessions.

19. You discover phone numbers, e-mail addresses or street addresses scribbled on scraps of paper or on the backs of business cards.

20. You find an undelivered or partially written love letter from him to his lover.

21. You find pictures of the two of them together.

22. He comes home with make-up or smudges of an unfamiliar shade of lipstick on his clothing. (Check his collar, sleeves, shoulders, the front of his shirt or jacket.)

23. There's a different brand of cigarettes from his or yours in the ashtray.

24. You see marks, symbols or notations in his appointment book or his calendar which indicate that he's tracking a woman's menstrual cycle. (First, make sure it's not yours.)

25. You find physical telltale signs in your home or car from unfamiliar restaurants, bars or clubs. (receipts, matchbooks, cocktail napkins, parking passes, business cards or other mementos or souvenirs)

26. Lipstick - stained cigarettes turn up in your home and you're a non-smoker.

27. You find deposit slips in his possession for someone else's bank account.

28. You find receipts, cancelled checks or money order stubs which indicate he's been paying his lover's bills.

29. You find evidence (deposit slips or bank statements) to indicate that he maintains a joint account with or for his lover.

30. You discover another woman's pictures, phone number, address, and/or e-mail address in his wallet or among his personal effects.

31. You find an article of clothing in your home that's not your size or style.

32. There are cigarette burns on the couch and both of you are non-smokers.

Chapter 26

HIS BEHAVIOR
AROUND OTHER WOMEN

Studies show that affairs are usually conducted with someone a man already knows—friends, neighbors, coworkers or business associates. If you're observant, you might be able to determine the identity of your husband's lover by the way he behaves in her presence, or by how she acts around him.

---

1. A certain female acts overly familiar with him.

2. He makes frequent or lengthy phone calls to a particular female "friend."

3. He acts extremely nervous or ill-at-ease in the presence of a particular female.

4. He goes to great lengths to avoid or ignore a woman with whom he was previously friendly.

5. He becomes unusually talkative or overly animated in the presence of a particular female. He literally "comes alive" when she's around.

6. He becomes uncharacteristically quiet or shy around a certain female.

7. He routinely discusses things with another female that he won't discuss with you.

8. When he's around a certain female, they exclude you from the conversation.

9. He gives a disproportionately expensive birthday or Christmas gift to his secretary, coworker, colleague or casual female "friend."

10. He knows entirely too much about a particular female's personal affairs.

11. He comes up with logical-sounding reasons or excuses to socialize with a certain female friend, neighbor or co-worker. Or he creates trumped-up reasons to visit her home, drop by her job, accompany her some place, or be in her presence, with or without you along.

12. He's overly curious about one of your girlfriends, a female neighbor or casual acquaintance.

13. He greets a woman unrelated to him with an overly affectionate hug or kiss.

14. His manners improve when he's in the presence of a particular woman. Suddenly he's a perfect gentleman.

15. He habitually discusses your marital problems with a close female friend.

16. He goes out of his way to do things for a female friend that he won't do for you.

17. He keeps encouraging you to cultivate a friendship with a particular female.

18. A certain female knows more than she should about your personal affairs.

19. He's always doing plumbing, painting, carpentry or electrical work (playing Mr. Fix-It) at a certain female's home.

20. He suggests or insists that you include a certain female in your social circle.

21. Your intuition tells you that a woman he's trying to pass off as a casual friend is really something more.

22. Whenever he's around a certain woman, he can't seem to stop smiling at her.

23. He becomes extremely attentive to or solicitous of a particular female.

24. He always calls the same female friend to share the special events in his life.

25. He displays a heightened energy around or responsiveness to a particular female.

26. He pays more attention to or shows more interest in another woman's children than he does his own.

27. Whenever a particular woman talks, he pays rapt attention, hanging onto her every word.

28. A certain woman calls him by a pet name.

29. He shares intimate details about his personal life with a particular female friend—things he's never revealed to anyone else but you.

30. You notice excessive or inappropriate gift-giving to (or from) a close friend of the opposite sex.

31. He always makes sexual innuendoes to or around a certain female.

32. A female friend always confers with him or calls him for advice.

33. A certain female suddenly becomes his main topic of conversation. He talks about her all the time–her activities, her habits, her likes and dislikes, her ideas, her opinions, etc.

34. You observe another woman touching him inappropriately.

35. You catch him winking or exchanging hand signals with another woman.

36. His behavior is "touchy-feely" or overtly sexual toward a particular female.

37. He and a certain female appear to be speaking in code to each other.

38. He's always doing favors for or giving little gifts to a certain female friend.

39. He appears to have more than a business relationship with a female co-worker or business associate.

40. When he's around a certain female, he can't seem to keep his eyes off her.

41. He habitually turns to the same female friend for emotional support.

42. He's always asking a particular female to do favors for him.

43. He ignores you completely (or tries to ignore you) whenever a certain female is around.

44. You overhear a woman make suggestive remarks to or about him.

45. He and another woman share a "private joke."

46. He suggests you wear your hair like, dress like, or otherwise imitate a particular woman.

47. He develops a sudden dislike for a woman you both know. (She may know about his affair.)

48. A particular female (neighbor, coworker, family friend) acts uncomfortable in your presence when he's around.

49. He always changes clothes or spruces himself up when he knows a certain female is coming by.

50. He becomes obsessed with a particular woman–asking all kinds of questions and trying to find out everything he can about her.

51. He has more to talk about with a female friend than he does with you.

52. He goes out of his way to impress a particular female— with his knowledge, talents, expertise or skills.

53. He suggests you invite your girlfriend, cousin, coworker or another female over for the weekend.

54. He accuses you of being jealous of a particular female.

55. He always compliments a particular female on her appearance.

56. His mood lifts whenever a certain female is around.

57. You catch him flirting (slyly or openly) with another woman.

58. You witness an exchange of phone numbers between him and another woman.

59. At a social event he spends an excessive amount of time in the company of a particular woman.

60. He has a female "friend" he calls several times a day.

61. He suddenly wants to leave a social gathering and go home when a certain female arrives.

62. You observe suspicious body language between him and a certain female.

63. Lately he's been overly critical of a particular female. (It may be a cover up for deeper feelings he has for her.)

64. At a social gathering, he consistently flirts with one particular woman.

65. He regularly repairs, maintains or services a particular female's car.

66. At a business function where spouses are invited you notice a certain tension in him when a female coworker comes over to say hello.

67. You observe another woman gazing at him lovingly or giving him adoring looks.

68. He's more courteous, mannerly, or gentleman-like to another woman than he is toward you. (Holding doors, carrying packages, helping with her coat, refreshing her drink, etc.)

69. He's always volunteering to mow a certain female neighbor's lawn.

70. The family dog acts overly familiar with a woman you don't know.

71. You keep running into the same woman when the two of you go out together. She always seems to turn up no matter where the two of you go.

Chapter 27

ACCIDENTAL SLIPS-UPS
OR DISCLOSURES

Sometimes you get lucky and find out what your husband has been up to through some strange quirk of fate. An accidental slip on his part or on the part of someone else can reveal what's been happening behind your back.

1. He accidentally calls you by her name in conversation—or worse yet—while making love to you.

2. The male friend he claimed to be hanging out with, calls or comes by looking for him.

3. While you're out with your girlfriends, you run into your husband with his lover.

4. You call his job to speak to him and find out he took the day off.

5. Someone who thought you already knew mentions the affair in your presence.

6. You find incriminating marks on his body that he didn't even realize he had.

7. He comes home from the store with receipts for a different day or time. (A man will sometimes have his lover make purchase several hours or several days in advance to support up his alibi that he "went to the store.")

8. When you mention the special project or all the overtime he's been working, his boss or coworkers give you a puzzled look.

9. He calls his lover's name in his sleep.

10. You run into him locally, when he was supposed to be out of town.

11. He mentions a restaurant, movie or play you enjoyed together, forgetting it was his lover he took, not you.

12. You find irrefutable evidence or proof that he inadvertently (or intentionally) left lying around (love letters, receipts, etc.).

13. He comes home wearing his underwear (or other article of clothing) inside out because he hastily dressed in the dark.

14. You find pictures of him with his lover.

15. A jealous or envious friend of his lover "blows the whistle" on them just for spite.

16. His lover's husband or boyfriend tells you about the affair hoping you put a stop to what's going on.

17. A well-meaning friend (or a busybody) decides to clue you in.

18. You wake up in the middle of the night and catch him sneaking out or trying to sneak back in.

19. A scorned lover, business rival or jealous male friend "spills the beans."

20. You pick up the phone to make a call and overhear an incriminating conversation between your husband and his lover.

21. A friend or acquaintance tells you that your husband was seen having lunch or dinner with a strange woman.

22. His friends complain that they never see him anymore, yet he claims to be hanging out with them.

23. When he gets on the elevator at home he frequently presses the same wrong button for a floor other than the one on which you live. (He's unconsciously pressing the button for his lover's floor.)

24. He claims to be going to the gym or health club to work out, but forgets to take his gym bag.

25. His carefully laid plans backfire and reveal what was going on behind your back.

26. Your female friends or acquaintances start regarding you with a look of pity—consistent with the wife being the last one to know.

27. His lover informs you that she's pregnant with his child.

28. You walk in on your husband and his lover having sex. If you find this telltale sign, it's the only sign you need.

29. You keep getting hints from well-meaning friends who know about his affair.

30. Someone who knows about his affair inadvertently reveals something that confirms your suspicions.

31. An incriminating instant message clearly intended for him pops up on the screen while you're online.

32. You catch him in a blatant lie.

33. His guilty conscience causes him to confess.

34. You call his hotel when he's out of town and you're told he's not registered there.

35. Your instinct tells you that something is just not right. Even experts agree that women seem to have a sixth sense when it comes to extramarital affairs. Trust your instinct or that internal radar that says something is wrong. If you have a strong gut feeling that he's cheating, he probably is.

36. Friends and family members start noticing things and keep asking if everything is okay between you two.

37. The dates, times, or addresses on receipts or ticket stubs don't coincide with his story.

38. You find out the night class or weekend class he claimed to be taking ended months ago.

39. You receive an anonymous letter giving you details about his affair.

40. His lover show ups at your door and tells you everything that's been going on.

41. He tells you he's working late but no one answers the phone at his office when you call.

42. Your child innocently clues you in to what's going on. (Sometimes men take very young children along with them to visit their lover, thinking the child is too young to understand what's going on.)

43. You call that suspicious number on your phone bill, and your husband answers the phone.

44. You find tangible evidence on the closet floor – phone numbers, receipts, love notes that have fallen out of his pants pocket. (Always check—this happens more frequently than you might think.)

45. You receive an anonymous phone call from someone who tells you about your husband's affair.

46. You find divorce papers he's had drawn up without your knowledge. (He's planning to spring them on you by surprise.)

47. You call his hotel room when he's out of town and a woman answers the phone.

48. You overhear him setting up an alibi with one of his friends.

49. You find out the restaurant, bar or club was closed at the time he says he was there.

50. He tells you he's going on a hunting, camping or fishing trip, but after he leaves you find his gear still in the closet, basement, or garage.

51. His lover sues him for child support.

52. You find out the event he said he attended was cancelled.

53. The workout clothes that he took to the gym come back fresh and unused.

54. He accidentally leaves an X-rated video in the VCR.

55. A coworker of his innocently inquires why you weren't at the event (company picnic, Christmas party) that your husband told you spouses couldn't attend.

56. You go to a new restaurant together and the waiter/waitress knows what he wants before he even places his order. (He obviously goes there regularly with someone else.)

57. He phones home but calls you by another woman's name. (He got his women or his phone numbers confused.)

PART III

Chapter 28

EVALUATING
WHAT YOU FOUND

How many telltale signs did you find? A few? Or a few dozen? One? Or a hundred? Be brutally honest with yourself about whatever you have (or haven't) found. If you didn't find very much, it's unwise (and unfair) to conclude that your husband is cheating on the basis of one or two random signs. There could be valid reasons why he's made a few changes in his life, or why he's altered his daily routine. A few telltale signs (depending on what they are) don't necessarily mean your husband is having an affair. In fact, many of these signs mean nothing in and of themselves. It's only when they appear in combination with other signs, that a suspicious pattern begins to form.

Telltale Signs Galore

What if you found an abundance of telltale signs? Pay close attention to the number, type, and significance of the telltale signs you found. Obviously, if you walked in on your husband having sex with someone else, that one sign is the only sign you need. If, over the course of several weeks, you find numerous telltale signs from several categories, you have valid cause for concern. The likelihood is very high that your husband is cheating, or he's in a "cheating frame of mind. For example, finding many telltale signs in the categories of physical appearance, telephone tip-offs, absences, how he relates to you and day-to-day behavior would be a sure indication that something's going on. The more telltale signs you find, the higher the probability is that your suspicions have been confirmed.

For Further Confirmation

If you need further confirmation or want more substantial evidence, it makes sense to hire a detective at this point. He can obtain details you were unable to get on your own. You might also want to hire a reputable investigator if you require court-admissible proof. He can monitor your husband's activities for several days (or weeks) and provide photos, videos, background checks (on the other woman), documented reports and any other information you may need. Cases are usually handled discreetly and with the strictest of confidence.

A Scarcity of Telltale Signs

What if, after a reasonable period of time, you found very few telltale signs? It could mean one of four things:

- Your husband is **not** cheating on you. Now you can get on with your life without a cloud of suspicion hanging over your marriage.

- Your suspicions were probably a figment of your imagination.

- You may be in denial. This can keep you from recognizing or acknowledging telltale signs that are probably obvious to everyone else. (Are you sure you really want to know the truth?)

- Your husband is an accomplished cheater or is highly skilled in the art of deception.

Hire A Pro

If you're still convinced that your husband is having an affair or if the last three situations apply to you, I strongly recommend that you get professional help. Hire a reputable private investigator. You need an expert who can conduct a more detailed investigation to substantiate or disprove those lingering suspicions you may have.

A RAY OF HOPE

Even if you find a multitude of telltale signs, things may not be as bad as they seem. It's highly possible that the affair hasn't actually happened yet. Instead of an affair in progress, you may have discovered a budding affair – one that has not yet taken place. Your husband could be strongly attracted to someone, but hasn't done anything about it yet. He may be simply toying with the idea of cheating for now – mentally weighing the pros and cons. He could be struggling with temptation or wracking his brain trying to figure out how he can pull it off. It's possible that he hasn't had a chance yet to carry out his adulterous plans.

Be thankful you've found out your husband's plans before any irreparable damage has been done to your marriage. Most women don't find out until it's too late. You have a unique opportunity to intervene in the situation and stop the affair before it begins. For guidance in doing this, refer to the booklet **"How to Affair-Proof Your Marriage."**

Chapter 29

YES, HE *IS* CHEATING – NOW WHAT?

The worst has happened. You've uncovered solid evidence that your husband is (or has been) cheating on you. Even if you suspected it all along, it's still traumatic to find out the truth. Few experiences in life are as painful as discovering that your husband is having an affair. Having personally experienced it, I know firsthand how devastating it is to learn that the man you love and trust has been seeing someone else.

Most wives are totally unprepared to cope with the emotional trauma of infidelity. After all, an affair isn't one of those life experiences you plan for in advance. Somehow you never envision something like this actually happening to you. When we take those marriage vows, we all visualize living "happily ever after."

Physical and Emotional Reactions

Let me warn you now about the tremendous physical and emotional upheaval you're about to undergo. You will find yourself suddenly overwhelmed by an uncontrollable torrent of mixed (and sometimes conflicting) emotions: shock, pain, disbelief, anger, shame, humiliation, guilt, self-blame, jealousy, bitterness, rage, and a desire for revenge.

The discovery of your husband's affair will take a physical toll on you as well. You may not be able to eat or sleep. Or you'll do too much of both. You'll cry constantly. Your stomach will be tied up in knots. Your blood pressure may rise. You may experience heart palpitations. The stress you're experiencing may even manifest itself as headaches, backaches or hives. You could become deeply depressed or experience anxiety attacks. Your immune system may decline, making you overly susceptible to colds or the flu. *What you're feeling is normal.* These are all common reactions when a woman discovers her husband's affair. Eventually these things will subside. Knowing what to expect may make it a bit easier to ride out the storm.

Use Your Support System

Now is the time to utilize the support system you put in place. Don't even think about trying to get through this alone. You need to talk with someone you trust about what you're going through. Don't worry about making any decisions right now. You need to first get your emotions under control. Right now your judgement will be seriously impaired by the powerful emotions you feel. Any decisions you make while in this state of mind will probably generate negative results. Let some of your pain subside before trying to take action of any kind.

What Not to Do

Knowing what not to do when your husband is cheating can be more important than knowing what to do. During the early phases of discovery, it's better to do nothing than to end up doing the wrong thing. Take your cue from an expression in the medical profession: "First, do no harm." Doing the wrong thing will only compound the problems you already have. For further guidance at this critical stage, get a copy of **"Mistakes to Avoid–What Not to Do when He's Cheating On You."**

Do Nothing You'll Later Regret

The most common mistake women make is acting out of panic. **Do *not* make any hasty decisions!** Your first impulse may be to leave your husband or put him out.

DON'T. Instead of your first move, this should be your last resort. If you still love your husband, don't abandon your marriage prematurely. You may later regret that you didn't try to work things out with the help of a marriage/family counselor, or at least reading a good book on coping with the aftermath of an affair. The way you handle the situation from the outset will determine whether you salvage your marriage or sabotage it. Be careful to avoid saying or doing things you may later regret. Be equally careful to avoid doing anything which will jeopardize you legally or financially. Dr. Carol Rhodes offers some excellent advice in her book, *Affairs, Emergency Tactics.*

There's Still Hope for Your Marriage

An affair doesn't automatically mean that your marriage is over. Many marriages can and do survive an affair. Handled the right way, the affair can be a turning point for strengthening your marriage. Together you and your husband can work to develop a new level of intimacy and trust. You have an opportunity to correct whatever has gone wrong in your marriage and deal with some of the problems the two of you may have overlooked. Many marriages have grown as a result of an affair. The way you handle this crisis will determine whether the affair is a death knell for your marriage or a wake-up call.

Find Out Why It Happened

Before you can make any decisions about what to do, you need to get a better understanding of why your husband cheated, and what this affair is all about. Whether you decide to stay with your husband or leave him, you need some insight as to what went wrong. Don't automatically blame yourself for what happened. Your husband's cheating is probably unrelated to anything you did or didn't do. It's true that a wife can sometimes unknowingly create an environment that fosters her husband's affair. But the problem usually starts with him, not you. As Dr. Bonnie Eaker Weil says in her book *Adultery, the Forgivable Sin,* "Take your share of the responsibility, but don't shoulder all the blame."

Your husband's cheating could be rooted in a life crisis he was undergoing at the time or it might be due to a major character flaw. Whatever the underlying reasons for his infidelity, the decision to cheat was his, not yours. He is responsible for his own behavior. For more insight on these aspects of infidelity, you might want to refer to **"Why Men Cheat—Situations that Cause Men to Cheat**" and **Is He the Cheating Kind?– How to Recognize a Cheater."**

You *Must* Confront Your Husband

The discovery of your husband's affair will mark a turning point in your marriage, for better or for worse. Which one will largely depend on you. Believing your marriage is over can turn into a self-fulfilling prophecy. So be optimistic about the end result.

I cannot stress strongly enough that an affair does **not** automatically mean your marriage has to end. Couples can successfully survive an affair. The confrontation is the key. This is the critical conversation in which you let your husband know that you're aware of his affair. You must have an in-depth discussion about it with him. During this discussion you'll ask him specific questions about what has occurred. His answers will help you decide what to do. Experts all agree that the first step to saving your marriage (and your sanity) is to tell your husband that you know about his affair.

Let me warn you in advance that it will not be an easy task. Plan your approach and carefully choose your words. Even so, this will be the most difficult conversation you and your husband will ever have. However, the two of you must openly and honestly discuss his affair if your marriage is to survive. Handled correctly, the confrontation gives you a strategic advantage and allows you to gather vital information. Postpone your decision-making until after this has been done. For detailed guidance and direction with this critical phase, get a copy of **"How to Confront your Husband About His Affair."**

> **NOTE:** If your husband is violent, do not confront him alone. Enlist the aid of a counselor, therapist, or religious advisor who is skilled at dealing with marital affairs.

Think Before You Act

After you confront your husband, give yourself time to think things through. Don't be in a hurry to make a decision – allow yourself at least several days. Carefully evaluate your situation. You need a well-thought-out plan. Before doing anything, consider the long-range effects of the decision you're about to make. Ask yourself these two questions for whatever you have in mind:

If I do this, what's the worst that can happen?

If I do this, what's the best outcome I can hope for?

Realize that you are capable of making good choices even in a bad situation. Weigh all your options before deciding which course of action to take.

Each Case is Different

Each case of infidelity is different. There's no one-size-fits-all solution when it comes to dealing with an affair. What worked for another couple might not work for you. While others may try to advise you, voice their opinions or offer suggestions about what you should do, you are the only one who can decide what's best for you. Only after you've explored all your options, can you proceed with a positive plan.

If You Decide to Stay

Not every marriage ends in divorce. You may decide to remain with your husband and try to work things out. It may be possible for the two of you to resolve the underlying problems that contributed to his affair. Today, there are a number of books available which offer helpful solutions and sound advice. Help is available. Don't feel that you have to do it alone. Studies indicate that couples who seek counseling are more likely to stay together. Things will always turn out better and go smoother and faster for you if you seek professional help. If you truly love your husband and he's willing to do his part, don't be afraid to follow your heart.

If You Decide to Leave

On the other hand, you may feel that divorce is the only solution for you. Not all marriages can be saved. If your marriage falls into this category, accept this fact and move on. Focus your efforts on preparing yourself financially and emotionally to bring your relationship to an end. But remember, even though your marriage may have ended, your life will still continue. It takes time, but you can pick up the pieces and build a new life for yourself.

It Takes Time

Whether you stay with your husband or leave him, it will not be an easy task. So don't expect overnight results. Let me remind you again, that it *will* take time, but you *can* get through this ordeal—with or without your husband. Thousands of women have done it and you can too. Know that you *can* heal from the wound of infidelity. Believe in yourself, hold your head high and let the healing begin.

COMING SOON!!
More Infidelity Titles
from
LIFESTYLE PUBLICATIONS

What Every Woman Should Know About Infidelity

Is He the Cheating Kind? – How to Recognize a Cheater

Why Men Cheat – Situations and Conditions that Cause Men to Cheat

Mistakes to Avoid – What Not to Do When He's Cheating On You

How To Confront Your Husband About His Affair

How to Affair-Proof Your Marriage

What to Do When He's Cheating on You – a 5 Point Plan

For more information on these titles,
visit our websites

www.LifestylePublications.com
www.Infidelity411.com
www.IsHeCheatingOnYou.com

or call
1-(800) 585 4905

E-mail:
IsHeCheatingBook@aol.com

REFERENCES

Amodeo, John. *Love & Betrayal.* New York: Ballantine Books a division of Random House, Inc.1994.

Baisden, Michael. *Never Satisfied How And Why Men Cheat.* Schaumburg, Illinois: Legacy Publishing. 1995.

Baroni, Diane & Kelly, Betty. *How To Get Him Back From The Other Woman.* New York: St. Martin's Press. 1992.

Bellafiore, Donna R. *Straight Talk About Betrayal.* Naperville, Illinois: DRB Alternatives Inc. 1999.

Blanchard, Paul. *Why Men Cheat And What To Do About It.* Tampa, Florida: Luv Books. 1995.

Botwin, Carol *Men Who Can't Be Faithful.* New York: Warner Books Inc. 1988.

Brown, Emily M. *Affairs: A Guide To Working Through The Repercussions Of Infidelity.* San Francisco, CA: Jossey-Bass Publishers. 1999.

Carder, Dave with Jaenicke, Duncan. *Torn Asunder.* Chicago Illinois: Moody Press. 1995.

Edell, Ronnie. *How To Save Your Marriage From An Affair.* New York: Kensington Pub Corp. 1990.

Green, Raymond B. *Cheating Mates.* New Brunswick Canada. 2000.

Harley Jr, Willard F. *H.I.S. Needs H.E.R. Needs:* Grand Rapids, MI: Baker Book House Pub. 1994.

Harley Jr, Willard F. and Chalmers, Jennifer Harley *Surviving An Affair.* Grand Rapids, MI: Baker Book House Company. 2000.

Harvey, Donald R. *Surviving Betrayal.* Grand Rapids, MI: Baker Books. 1995.

Hopson, Derek S. and Hopson, Darlene Powell. *Friends, Lovers, And Soul Mates.* New York: Simon and Schuster. 1994.

Kelley, Susan *Why Men Stray Why Men Stay.* Halbrook, MA: Adams Media Corporation. 1996.

Lee,Virginia *Affairs of the Heart.* Freedom, CA: The Crossing Press. 1993.

Linquist, Luann. *Secret Lovers.* San Francisco, CA: Jossey-Bass Inc., Publishers. 1989.

Louise, Jay D *How To Have An Affair And Never Get Caught.* Fort Lauderdale, Florida: Roxan Books 1995.

Lusterman, David. *Infidelity a Survival Guide.* Oakland, CA: New Harbinger Publications. 1998.

Pittman, Frank. *Private Lies.* New York: W. Norton & Company. 1990.

Rhodes, Carol L. *Affairs Emergency Tactics.* Rochester Hills, MI: Somerset Publishing. 1999.

Simone, Ferne and Sheen, Sammi. *Is He Cheating?.* New York: Berkley Books. 1998.

Spring, Janis Abrams. Ph.D. *After the Affair.* New York: Harper Perennial a division of Harper Collins. 1996.

Squires, Kelly. *Spying On Your Spouse.* Secaucus, NJ: Citadel Press. 1997.

Staheli, Lana. *Triangles.* New York: Harper Collins Publishers Inc. 1997.

Subotnik, Rona M. & Gloria Harris. *Surviving Infidelity.* Adams Publishing Halbrook, Ma. 1994.

Vaughan, Peggy. *The Monogamy Myth* .New York: Newmarket Press. 1989.

Warren, Sally with Thompson, Andrea. 1998. *Dumped!.* New York: Harper Paperbacks. 1999

Weber, Eric and Simring, Steven S.*How to Win Back the One You Love.* New York: Bantam Books. 1983.

Weil, Bonnie Eaker. *Adultery The Forgivable Sin* New York: Carol Publishing Group. 1993.

Weiner, Marcella Bakur and DiMele, Armand. *Repairing Your Marriage After His Affair.* Rocklin, CA: Prima Publishing. 1998.

Weiner, Marcella Bakur and Starr, Bernard D. *Stalemates.* Far Hills, New Jersey: New Horizon Press. 1991.

Wirsche, Alda & Milot, Marnie. *Gotcha*!!! Toronto. Ontario: Uphill Publishing LTD. 1998.

INDEX

Share Your Story

My research on infidelity is an ongoing process. If you are (or have been) a victim of infidelity and would like to share your story with me, feel free to do so at:

My Story@IsHeCheatingOnYou.com

Your information will be held in strict confidence. Or you may send your story anonymously, if you prefer. I welcome any comments, questions, or suggestions you may have. Please contact me directly at:

RuthHouston@IsHeCheatingOnYou.com

ABOUT THE AUTHOR

Ruth Houston is a lifestyle writer/editor whose articles on relationships, fashion, beauty, fitness and travel and "Good Loving" column have appeared regularly for the past 18 years in publications in the United States and abroad. She is a member of the American Society of Journalists and Authors and is listed in Working Press of the Nations, Bacon's Media Bank and Gales Consultants and Consulting Organizations.

A former fashion editor with a diversified background in beauty and fashion, Ms. Houston has also worked as public relations manager and spokesperson for Clairol, executive editor for *Fashion World,* fashion columnist for *Entrepreneurial Woman,* and director of training for Rubi Cosmetics. She holds a degree in Advertising and Communications from the Fashion Institute of Technology in New York.

Ms. Houston has been a frequent guest on Good Day New York and other TV and radio talk shows nationwide discussing male/female relationships and related lifestyle topics. She is available for speaking engagements.

Having been a victim of infidelity herself, Ms. Houston firmly believes that every woman should learn to recognize the telltale signs of infidelity. Her motto is **"Don't speculate – investigate. Find out before it's too late."** She is happily re-married and lives in New York with her husband, Manley and their nine cats. She can be contacted at

P.O. Box 730797,
Elmhurst, New York, 11373
e-mail
CheatingSigns@aol.com
RuthHouston@IsHeCheatingOnYou.com.

To Order

Additional copies of
Is He Cheating On You? - 829 Telltale Signs
can be ordered from our website at
www.IsHeCheatingOnYou.com

- -

Telephone Orders
(Toll free)
1-800-585-4905
or
1-877-829-SIGNS

Please have your credit card ready.

- -

Fax Orders
718-592-2018
Use form on opposite page

Order extra copies as gifts for your female friends and relatives.

Please send me _____ copies of *Is He Cheating On You?-829 Telltale Signs* at $29.95 each. Please add $4.95 postage and handling for each book. All orders are sent by Priority Mail.

Name: _____

Address: _____

City: _____ State _____ Zip _____

Telephone: _____

Email: _____

My ☐ check   ☐ money order for _____ is enclosed.

Please make check or money order payable to Lifestyle Publications.

Please charge my   ☐ Visa   ☐ MasterCard

Card Number: _____

Exp. Date: _____

Signature: _____

Lifestyle Publications
P.O. Box 730797
Elmhurst, New York 11373
1-800-585-4905

www.IsHeCheatingOnYou.com

Did we leave out any telltale signs?

If you know of any telltale sign that we missed, e-mail us at
TelltaleSigns@IsHeCheatingOnYou.com
and we'll include them in the next edition of this book.

I Knew He was Cheating When...

How did you discover your husband's infidelity? What finally convinced you he was cheating on you? Share your story with us at:

MyStory@IsHeCheatingOnYou.com

Get Your
Infidelity Questions
Answered

__www.Infidelity411.com__

Everything you need to know about infidelity
from discovery to recovery

If you borrowed this book, order your own personal copy using the order form below:

Please send me _____ copies of *Is He Cheating On You?- 829 Telltale Signs* at $29.95 each. Please add $4.95 postage and handling for each book. All orders are sent by Priority Mail.

Name: _____

Address: _____

City: _____ State _____ Zip_____

Telephone: _____

Email: _____

My ☐ check   ☐ money order for _____ is enclosed.

Please make check or money order payable to Lifestyle Publications.

Please charge my   ☐ Visa   ☐ MasterCard

Card Number: _____

Exp. Date: _____

Signature: _____

Lifestyle Publications
P.O. Box 730797
Elmhurst, New York 11373
1-800-585-4905

www.IsHeCheatingOnYou.com

COMING SOON!!
More Infidelity Titles
from
LIFESTYLE PUBLICATIONS

What Every Woman Should Know About Infidelity

*Is He the Cheating Kind? – How to
Recognize a Cheater*

*Why Men Cheat – Situations and Conditions
that Cause Men to Cheat*

*Mistakes to Avoid – What Not to Do When
He's Cheating On You*

How To Confront Your Husband About His Affair

How to Affair-Proof Your Marriage

*What to Do When He's Cheating on You –
a 5 Point Plan*

Join our mailing list for updates on these titles.

Name _____

Address _____

City _____ State _____ Zip _____

Telephone: _____

E-mail: _____

LIFESTYLE PUBLICATIONS P.O. Box 730797 Elmhurst, NY 11373
1-(800) 585 4905 E-mail: IsHeCheatingBook@aol.com

Or visit our websites:
www.LifestylePublications.com • www.Infidelity411.com

Order Form

Please send me _____ copies of *Is He Cheating On You?- 829 Telltale Signs* at $29.95 each. Please add $4.95 postage and handling for each book. All orders are sent by Priority Mail.

Name: _____

Address: _____

City: _____ State _____ Zip _____

Telephone: _____

Email: _____

My ☐ check   ☐ money order for _____ is enclosed.

Please make check or money order payable to Lifestyle Publications.

Please charge my   ☐ Visa   ☐ MasterCard

Card Number: _____

Exp. Date: _____

Signature: _____

Lifestyle Publications
P.O. Box 730797
Elmhurst, New York 11373
718-592-6039
1-877-829-SIGNS
1-800-585-4905

Email:
IsHeCheatingbook@aol.com
Orders@IsHeCheatingOnYou.com